Thomas D. Christie.
Nov. '62 .

The new small garden

The new small garden

Lady Allen of Hurtwood, F.I.L.A.

and Susan Jellicoe

THE ARCHITECTURAL PRESS LONDON

Printed in Great Britain by Staples Printers Ltd. at their Rochester, Kent, establishment and first published by the Architectural Press, London, 1956.

Contents

Acknowledgements

The preparation of a book of this kind was only made possible by the enthusiasm and interest of the owners, not only of the gardens shown, but also of many other gardens which it was not found possible to include. The authors would like to record their gratitude and to include in their thanks the many people who gave invaluable advice and encouragement.

They are particularly indebted to those gardeners who drew their own plans, namely: B. L. Adams (page 98); Dr. A. Auer, Head of the City Parks Department, Vienna (page 87); Derek Bridgwater (page 76); Neville Conder (page 116); Jeremy Dodd (page 37); Frederick Gibberd (page 60); Barbara Jones (page 29); Graham Lang (page 72); Eywin Langkilde (page 56); Alan Reiach (page 105); John Sutcliffe (page 42, section and perspective); Herbert Tayler and David Green (page 33). Hugo Boyd drew the remainder of the plans. Some of these were based on preliminary drawings kindly provided by K. Bourne (page 95); Brenda Colvin (pages 102 and 109); Anthony Denney (page 88); John Lacey (page 84); Brian Peake (page 70); J. Sturk (page 50).

Grateful acknowledgement is made to the following photographers: B. L. Adams (pages 97 and 101); Derek Bridgwater (page 77 top and bottom); Neville Conder (page 119); H. de Burgh Galwey (page 71 top and bottom); Anthony Denney (pages 89, 90 top); Jeremy Dodd (page 38); Percy Flaxman (page 20); Foto-Bayer (by courtesy of Otto Valentien) (pages 14, 123 bottom); Frederick Gibberd (page 64 left and right); Eduard Ihm (page 123 top); John Ingleby (page 59); Eywin Langkilde (page 57 top and bottom); Helmut Partaj (by courtesy of Dr. A. Auer) (pages 86, 87); Gordon Patterson (page 74 left and right); Percy Pitt (page 73 top and bottom); Alan Reiach (pages 106, 107, 108 left and right); Michael Russell (page 122 top right); John Sutcliffe (page 41); Stephen Sykes (page 15); Herbert Tayler and David Green (pages 31, 33, 34, 35, 36); Julian Trevelyan (page 25 bottom); H. Wainwright (pages 62, 63). All other photographs were taken by Susan Jellicoe.

6

This illustrated book of small gardens has been prepared in the hope that it will be stimulating and helpful to those who would like to design and make their own garden, but who may not be quite sure what effect they would like to achieve or how they should set about their task.

The gardens selected are not imaginary ones; they actually exist and all but three have been made by the owners themselves who, in the course of evolving their ideas, have made their mistakes before reaching pleasant and satisfying successes.

Some people who are not trained in reading the meaning behind a drawn plan of a garden are often baffled. The authors have tried to make the essential plan easily understandable by taking photographs from different aspects in each garden to bring the plan to life for the reader and to emphasize certain features that are thought to be of interest or of importance to the design as a whole.

The symbolic man stretched alongside the scale will perhaps help the reader better to visualize the size of each garden.

All the gardens shown in this book are small; some are in towns, others on new housing estates in the country. A few have been selected from other countries where the climate is comparable with that of Great Britain and the problems similar to those faced by the owners of a new plot or by those wishing to reconstruct their existing gardens.

*   *   *

In the search for charming gardens that were appropriate and interesting the authors found that many small gardens showed obvious signs of being unpremeditated and haphazard, as though the owners had not, perhaps, had the time to sit down and consider what kind of garden it was that they would really like to have. Those gardens which gave the owner and his family the most pleasure – the ones that had an air of being right – were simple in design and of good proportions.

It is all too easy to say that good design depends on good proportions, but ever since classical times people have been trying to define what they mean by good proportion. No rule-of-thumb guidance can safely be given here, but only pictorial examples that may help to clarify the essence of good proportion. This elusive quality can best be studied

7

from the plans and is most easily seen from those on pages 60, 84 and 116. Some gardens that are satisfying have certainly been evolved almost by a happy chance, which perhaps bears out the saying of Lord Melbourne that 'much of what is attributed to design is accident; the unknown cause leading to the unknown end'. An amateur is, in this respect, really on a level with the professional designer, because the end result will ultimately depend on a multitude of influences that have moulded the sensibilities of the person creating the garden. He may well have been influenced, though unconsciously, by what he saw and enjoyed in childhood, by what he has read in books or seen in a neighbour's garden or by an association of ideas that he has carried with him from travels abroad. A plan may be well conceived and carried out with technical 'expertise' and yet the result may be plain boring unless the whole is enriched by a sensitive feeling for plants and materials and the general fitness of things. The result will certainly be dull if the ordering is dull, however technically correct the whole conception.

A garden, and a small one in particular, is a place where one can retire from the outside world as into a private study, there to enjoy a feeling of quiet contentment. Edward Kemp, a landscape gardener writing in the middle of the nineteenth century, says in his book *How to Lay Out a Garden*, 'Few characteristics of a garden contribute more to render it agreeable than *snugness* and *seclusion*. They serve to make it appear peculiarly one's own, converting it into a kind of *sanctum*. . . .Those who love their garden often want to walk, work, ruminate, read, romp or examine the various changes of Nature in it, and to do so unobserved.'

It will be seen from the gardens which follow that there has been a willingness to accept the conditions imposed, whether of size, soil, aspect or the trials of acid-polluted air. A problem to be faced by all small-garden owners is how best to include what is wanted without fuss and to resist the temptation to over-elaborate. The too-ambitious garden is usually less effective and restful than one based on a simple plan that is appropriate to the size of the house and yet manages to meet the needs of the family. This does not necessarily mean that the whole garden is seen at the first glance – the challenge to one's skill comes in evolving a design that has a slight mystery about it and some of that valuable quality in a garden – surprise. No garden of crudely staring beds, ostentatious and regimented planting can ever be so restful as one in which every

An outdoor sitting space.

plant looks at home, where every pace brings a surprise and fresh interest. Character, a somewhat indefinable quality, can probably only be obtained by having an overall aim in mind, and then doing one thing at a time as clearly as possible, thereby avoiding confusion and complexity. The proper use of changes of level, screens and appropriate planting all help to give this quality. Success is usually the result of not attempting too much.

The problem of ordering the space at one's disposal so as to satisfy the intellect and at the same time crystallize the ideas that have been absorbed is, indeed, the essence of the task. Since the space available will certainly be contained within a boundary of some kind, whether brick walls, a hedge or the daunting chain-link fencing, a decision will

9

have to be taken as to how the boundaries are to be treated. Where the garden is to be regarded as an additional room, without its ceiling, and where one wishes to be deliberately aware of the limitation of size, the walls can be decorated and used as part of the design. This has been done in the office garden (page 46) and in the first of the two long gardens (page 60). Alternatively, if there is a wish to be unaware of confinement, an attempt can be made to plant out the boundary, as in the garden near Sloane Square (page 52) and the shrub garden at Crawley (page 49), so that the eye does not apprehend too clearly the true size of the garden. In the second of the two long gardens (page 65) there is a combination of these two ideas. The side walls are here used for decoration and yet the green planting behind the trellis at the end gives the illusion that the garden goes on indefinitely. Although the rational side of our nature is not deceived, the mind can delude itself almost endlessly and by resort to such subterfuges fancy can freely wander outside the physical boundary of the garden.

Those who would extract all possible pleasure and beauty from their gardens should become, not gardeners only, but students of beautiful form, for it is essentially in a confined space, without the distraction of a rolling landscape or distant view, that the essence of shape, form, colour and texture of an individual plant can best be appreciated and enjoyed.

In a large country garden with a wide sky and broad landscape it is not improvident to neglect some of the abundant opportunities. But in a small garden, whether in town or country, every chance should be taken to enhance perception in all possible ways. There are not only the ground and the walls to be considered; there is also the sky to be enjoyed. There is much pleasure in lying flat on the lawn or in a hammock the better to contemplate the movement of clouds or the silhouette of trees and leaves against the light. Here is a fresh aspect of the garden which can make an added contribution to its more total use. Incidentally, it may also be the only way in towns to cut buildings out of the view so as to feel really engulfed in a garden. In the Scandinavian countries much use is made of outdoor fires where impromptu meals can be cooked. A glowing fire is especially attractive when placed within a partially protected area for added comfort. Not only are these fires decorative in a garden setting, but they also lengthen the time that the garden can be enjoyed. Similarly, lighted candles on a garden table or

An atmosphere of mystery and illusion can be introduced into a tiny garden.

pedestal on a summer evening can be entrancing. Discreetly placed lights bring a magical new look to familiar plants and flowers and are easily arranged with an insulated cable. To find ways and means to extend the time when a small garden can be enjoyed is an absorbing pleasure.

It was perhaps surprising that the authors failed to find a small garden devoted, at least in part, to flowers that bloom in the late evening and night. Many gardens are used these busy times only after the day's work is past when the pleasure from these nocturnal flowers is great. The possible variety is considerable and most of them are fragrant and white, otherwise it would be difficult for them to attract the moths that fertilize them and for whom the most fragrant scents are evolved. Red flowers

11

Difficult conditions are a challenge to ingenuity.

are amongst the earliest to close and very few of the really blue flowers
are scented. Some of the gardens in this book would perhaps have gained
added interest if the scentless shrubs and flowers had been replaced by
others equally suitable and beautiful, but with the added attraction of
fragrance. It is by no means impossible, even in a town, to have scented
flowers in the garden the whole year through, if it is remembered that
those which bloom in the winter and the very early spring like to have
protection in the rough weather.

Much labour and gardening effort is wasted in trying to grow flowers
in an inappropriate position, and often a better sense of serenity and
beauty may be achieved by the use of paving. The wise selection of the
right tree, shrub or plant for particular positions requires both know-

12

ledge and a touch of inspiration. The first essential is that they should be suited horticulturally for the soil and aspect in which they will spend their lives. A good look round the neighbouring gardens will often give a guide as to plants that flourish. Much valuable information may be had from the sources given in the Appendix 'How to find out' (page 127) as to varieties, planting and culture. When the opportunity offers, it is worth considering the use of trees or shrubs that might have a double purpose and so extend their interest. In the Zürich garden (page 20) the trees have been selected to give not only shade, but fruit as well. How much more charming this is than, say, an ornamental cherry which goes ice-pink for a couple of days and is then finished for the season. Hedges, too, need not be a dead loss if there is a willingness to forget the privet and *Thuya Lobbii* and to experiment instead with shrub roses or to intermingle climbing roses with existing planted boundaries, as in the tapestry hedge described on page 35. The use of informal mixed planting to disguise the boundaries is well shown in the garden at Strand-on-the-Green (page 112).

Many town dwellers are blessed with the best of all small-garden boundaries – a brick wall, which can in itself be a thing of beauty when it has acquired its mellowing *patina*. It not only gives visual protection and a pleasant sense of calm enclosure, but serves to protect the plants and humans alike from irritating draughts and winds. The hard lines of the walls are, however, always better for being clothed, since the English mind does not like complete finality. Where neither hedge nor wall is appropriate or available, a carefully designed trellis or bamboo screen takes up little room and may serve also as a good support for climbers.

William Morris, writing in *Hopes and Fears for Art*, says: 'Large or small, the garden should look both orderly and rich . . . it should by no means imitate either the wilfulness or the wilderness of Nature, but should look like a thing never seen except near a house.' Perhaps not all will agree with William Morris, especially those who have an urge to bring the country into the confined space of an urban garden as an antidote to living in a city. If attempted, it may be one of the most difficult things to do successfully, just because Nature cannot be copied or the planning learned by rote. The deliberate disarray of the green parlour on page 27 is uniquely successful in this respect. Nevertheless, the enjoyment of a garden, which should be both convenient and inviting, will largely depend upon its good relationship to the house. The

13

Bamboo screens provide seclusion, as well as support for climbers and ramblers.

view from the windows should also be considered, for the contemplation of a garden from inside the house is both pleasurable and instructive. It will be from the house or from the terraced platform, which should be considered as part of the house, that the modelling of a garden and the change of levels will be most apparent, and the problem of creating a good balance between the different parts will be all important. The owner of the Highgate garden (page 83) has deliberately made a garden that is clearly defined. Because the relationship between the different areas is sound, the shapes satisfying, and each compartment has its own kind of furnishing, the subconscious mind is at peace. It may be some guide to consider the idea that it is generally more restful when one material, such as paving, clearly predominates over another material,

14

Seen from within, the garden should offer an invitation.

such as grass, or vice versa. When these two materials or other dominant textures are used in the proportion of fifty-fifty, the result will probably be indecisive and unsatisfactory.

The happy garden is one that can be fully used by all members of the family, and this will probably be the starting point when one is contemplating the layout. The baby in the pram should have a sheltered spot, perhaps under a tree that he can watch, and his older sister will enjoy playing in a sand trough on dry paving sufficiently spacious for her to arrange her toys in the sun. If the living-room leads into the garden, a paved or brick terrace will make it easy to extend its boundaries and make an outdoor room for meals or for sitting at ease between household duties.

Another basic consideration before a start is made will most certainly be the probable initial cost of making the garden and the ease of upkeep. It is perhaps not without interest to say that only two of the gardens in this book depend on outside help for maintenance. Once a simple and appropriate design has been decided upon and, if possible, drawn to scale for guidance, the main paths, flower and vegetable beds can be pegged out and a beginning made with construction.

It is a pleasant thought that gardens can be more easily adjusted than a house and the wise gardener will add his embellishments slowly as the whole scheme takes shape. The purpose of this book is not to present to the reader ready-made plans to be slavishly copied, or to impart technical knowledge that can be found in garden books, but rather to stimulate thought and to indicate some good ideas that have proved to be satisfying. It is often supposed that the small plot gives little scope for invention or deliberate design. It is in the hope that this theory may be disproved that this book has been prepared.

A decorative corner near the coalshed.

A Country Garden in St. John's Wood, London

A plain rectangular garden, sixty feet by thirty, enclosed by high brick walls, is a familiar problem to many who live in a town. Lady (Kythe) Hendy constructed this garden entirely herself without any outside help. She has shown her wisdom by concentrating the rich herbaceous planting on the sunny side and has added extra depth of soil by constructing a twelve-inch dry stone wall. On the shady side of the garden is a narrow border, thick with forsythia, syringa, clematis and roses that climb up and over the wall.

What was the old scullery has been opened up to form a loggia that leads onto the paved sitting space, and this in turn is linked to the garden by tubs planted with catmint (*Nepeta Mussini*). A luxuriant pear tree covers the somewhat dull house wall, with its main stem acting as its own support. The tables, chairs and tubs are painted Atlantic green.

Overlooking this simple garden, with its country-like exuberance, is a small roof garden leading out of the first-floor sitting-room. Here again, all is simplicity, with runner beans making an effective pattern up the partition wall, tomatoes in tubs facing the sun and tobacco plants (*nicotiana*) filling the evening air with perfume.

Lady Hendy attributes her success to compost (see page 124), which she considers more precious than gold, and to the free use of lime. The flower borders receive a generous sprinkling of slaked lime at least once a year and are further helped with mulches of compost from time to time and dressings of National Growmore fertilizer.

It is rare for town plants to be as happy as those that grow in the country. They are mostly more difficult to establish and they do not increase with the same exuberance. It is by no means easy to decide what plants to select for a small garden and because space is so precious it is necessary to be ruthless in discarding plants that are obviously unhappy. Lady Hendy has succeeded through a painful process of trial and error. Now she uses only perennial plants which lose their leaves in the winter. Nearly all rock plants which hold their leaves get clogged with soot and, in the end, fail. This applies to the thymes, pinks, carnations, aubrietia, rock roses and alyssum. Rosemary, lavender and the conifers, with their glaucous leaves that the rain cannot clean, also dis-

Above: the pink walls make an excellent foil for the pear.
Right: a carved wooden figure bought for a song in a Piccadilly store, where it had been used for displaying table linen. It has been placed in the herbaceous border with a charmingly casual effect.

like a sooty atmosphere. Lady Hendy has found annuals and biennials difficult to raise from seed and now buys them as young plants in the spring. Bulbs usually do well their first year, with the possible exception of tulips, but they also tend to diminish and go blind in succeeding years. She believes that many town gardeners get discouraged just because they fail to accept the fact that they must replenish their stocks from time to time. The problem in the country is that one must always be thinning out and discarding crowded material; in towns, because some plants tend to diminish in size, renewal may be necessary from time to time.

The house walls are coloured a warm pink which makes an excellent foil for the pear and gives a pleasant 'southern' feeling to the garden. The walls were first conscientiously cleaned with a long-handled scrubbing brush dipped in detergent and afterwards they were rinsed in clean water. The colour was made from plastic emulsion white paint, tinted with scarlet and chrome-yellow water-bound stainers. Any good colour

merchant will give wise advice on mixing and how best to apply. In this case the colour has worn well and improved with age.

MATERIALS

Paving Random rectangular York stone.

Trees Flowering Japanese double Cherry (*Prunus serrulata sekiyana* [*Kanzan*]); Pear; Siberian Crab Apple (*Malus baccata*).

Shrubs *Clematis montana rubens*; Forsythia; Honeysuckle (*Lonicera fragrantissima*); Mock Orange Blossom (*Philadelphus*); Yellow Winter Jasmine (*Jasminum nudiflorum*); White Jasmine (*Jasminum officinale*).

Roses Climbers, rather difficult to establish, but good after a slow start. Dwarf polyantha and sweet briar, good but rather subject to mould.

Herbaceous Perennials Catmint (*Nepeta Mussini*); Dahlias; Day Lilies (*Hemerocallis*); Delphiniums; Helenium; Hollyhocks (self-seeding); Iris; Lily of the Valley; Lupins; Paeonies; Periwinkle (*Vinca minor*); *Salvia haematodes*; Sidalcea; Solomon's Seal.

Vegetables are often looked upon as a kind of horticultural Cinderella, to be pushed out of sight behind a trellis or a row of espalier fruit trees. And they can certainly look ugly and untidy. That it need not always be so is shown by this engagingly simple Swiss garden, whose charm depends largely on the way the vegetables are mixed up with the rest of the garden. They take up quite half the garden and there is no suggestion that they are anything to be ashamed of. In fact, the pattern made by their trim rows is an important ingredient in the design of the garden.

Large clumps of perennials such as phlox and oriental poppies have been planted near the house and at one or two points near the path, where they catch the eye and break up the rigidity and neatness of the vegetables. The *Megasea cordifolia* near the gate looks perfectly at home next to the currant bushes and rhubarb plants. Otherwise flowers are restricted to narrow strips in front of the two boundaries. The bed on the north side is raised up about eighteen inches, owing to a change in the level of the soil, and here rock plants and nasturtiums make a line of strong colour.

Plenty of provision is made for relaxation, either on the sunny terrace and grass lawn near the house or on the small grass strip under the shade of the damson tree. Near-by, a seat in an arbour offers seclusion as well as shade.

Left: the social centre of the garden – a seat on the left under the arbour and a lawn beneath the trees on the right of the path.
Right: home-made paving stones such as these can be made to look more mature by brushing over them skim milk or thin manure water. Both these encourage the growth of algae and minute fungi which take away the rawness.

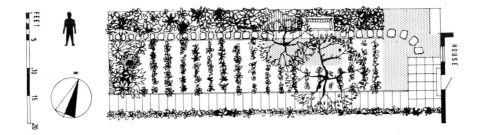

A Riverside Garden in Chiswick

From a study of the plan alone, this garden would appear to be formal, but in reality, although the 'bones' of the design are regular, the skilled placing of individual plants of character has given the narrow entrance garden and the outdoor-living garden an air of bohemian casualness.

The artist owners, Julian Trevelyan and his wife, Mary Fedden, had two thoughts uppermost in their mind; to have a garden that would look after itself when they were away for long periods abroad, and a garden suited to sociable living. They were faced with the need for getting rid of a substantial quantity of surplus rubble and rubbish, and rather than meet the cost of having it carted away (always an expense in towns), they used it to create interesting changes of level. Much of it was used to make the raised platform in the corner, which gives a view down river and serves as a shady terrace for tables and benches. To vary the levels in a small garden is a happier solution for disposing of rocks and bricks than using them to make the all too familiar pseudo-rock garden. A rock garden, by its very nature, should be associated with an open landscape, and perhaps one of the secrets of good taste, as shown in this garden, is that the conception should be appropriate to the circumstances. The grass plots and flower beds are all raised above the home-made, random rectangular paving, edged with old brick.

It is a collector's garden in the sense that most of the plants have been raised from seeds and cuttings gathered in other countries, from the gardens of friends or from the hedgerows. Full value is given to plants that have beautiful shape and foliage; it could be said, in fact, that the stately giant cow parsnip or the mullein with its towering candelabra of flowers, are treated almost like pieces of sculpture to give a sense of form and emphasis. An interesting comparison can be made between this garden and that of Barbara Jones (page 27). Both depend on appreciation of plant form, but whereas Miss Jones chooses to arrange her plants so that the shape and texture of one acts as a foil to others, Mr. Trevelyan is not so much concerned with the juxtaposition of plants as with an appreciation of the value of the form of the individual plant.

Being artists with a cosmopolitan background, Mr. and Mrs. Trevelyan naturally enjoy good food and although they have no room for growing

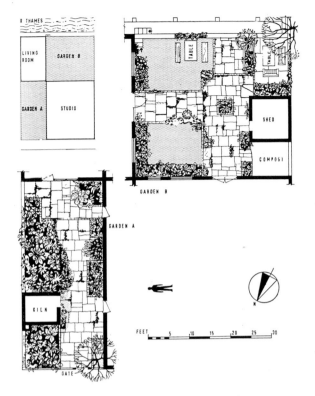

vegetables, full use has been made of the soil between the paving stones to grow many herbs. The bold, branching flower stems and the finely cut foliage of the common fennel are not only a decoration in the garden and in the house, when cut, but are used in sauces or as a garnish. Mint, various thymes, basil, tarragon and chervil, a bush of sage and a clump of marjoram are all herbs that grow well in such a situation.

Both the entrance garden and the living garden depend largely on plants with restful grey-green leaves, such as the *Cistus purpureus* with its familiar Mediterranean scented foliage, plantain lily and the stately plume poppy, which likes to be planted in partial shade so that its leaves have shelter and the strong inflorescences can grow into the brighter light above. The grey-leaved *Alyssum saxatile, Sedum cauticolum* with its blueish-grey waxy leaves, and other small plants billow out informally over the paving. In the entrance garden a *Clematis montana rubens* throws its pink flowers over the kiln and can be enjoyed over the top of the six-foot wall by passers-by. On the boundary wall of the entrance garden a sweetwater vine grows freely and once produced thirty-eight pounds of white grapes to make sixteen bottles of home-

23

Left: the entrance garden, leading from the road to the living-room (A on plan) The plants on the right, mostly in shade, are herbs and other grey-green leafed plants, culminating in the dramatic group of giant cow parsnip.

Below: immediately to the left inside the gate is an essay in colour and texture, with a *Clematis Nelly Moser* climbing over an old tree stump as the central feature.

Above right: A general view of the inner garden (B on plan).

Below right: lunch on the raised terrace overlooking the Thames.

Seen from the studio, the mullein has the quality of sculpture. The fennel beside it sends up a fountain of feathery leaves.

made wine. Outdoor vines, if they are to fruit well, need a sunny aspect, adequate drainage and good fibrous loam to start them off. As they are gross feeders it is well to fortify them with well-decayed farm-yard manure and coarse bone meal. A good substitute for farm-yard manure, which is by no means easy to get in towns, is well-rotted compost, and it will be noticed that Mr. Trevelyan has made provision for his compost-heap in a corner of the outdoor-living garden.

MATERIALS

Paving Rectangular concrete slabs (home-made); old London bricks.

Trees Plum; Willow (dwarf).

Shrubs Buddleia; *Cistus purpureus*; *Clematis montana rubens* and *Nelly Moser*; *Daphne mezereum* (both white and pink); Fig; Honeysuckle (*Lonicera*); Ivies (mixed with rambler roses); Magnolia; Vine (Sweetwater).

Roses Ramblers.

Herbaceous Perennials Cow Parsnip (*Heracleum mantegazzianum*); Iris; Mullein (*Verbascum Broussa*); Plantain Lily (*Hosta grandiflora*); Plume Poppy (*Bocconia cordata*); Valerian (*Centranthus ruber atrococceus*); Herbs.

Alpines *Alyssum saxatile*; *Dianthus caesus plenus* and *deltoides* (Wisley var.); *Gentiana septemfida* (not too happy); *Geranium Pylzowianum*; *Phlox subulata Betty* and *subulata Temiscaming*; *Saxifraga lingulata Albertii*; *Sedum cauticolum*; Thymes.

This exquisite little garden has been evolved by Miss Barbara Jones, artist and writer, from as unprepossessing a back yard as can be imagined. It is essentially a collector's garden, where each plant is valued as an individual. The tiny scale (so small that the symbolic man could not be used on the plan because he would have taken too much room) makes the individual treatment of plants not only appropriate but necessary. It is her delight to arrange her plants so that the shape and texture of each will act as a sympathetic foil to its neighbours.

Miss Jones's list of plants is given in detail on page 29, just because it is an amusing reflection of the way in which she has set about the creation of this microcosm.

A world within a world.

Above: Barbara Jones likes to have one or two objects that are *nature morte.* Under the arbour is a beautiful piece of silvery dead tree trunk.

Below: in a really small garden such as this it is important to have at least one large plant to prevent it from becoming pretty-pretty. The heracleum should, however, be cut down after flowering, otherwise it gets untidy and tends to be smothered in black fly.

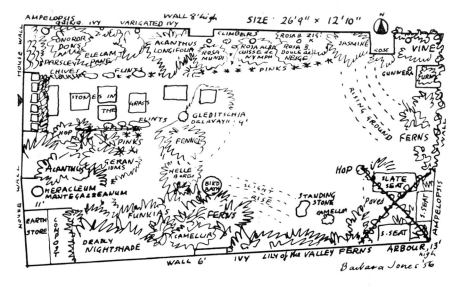

A CATALOGUE OF PLANTS, TOOLS, ETC.

	£	s.	d.
Ampelopsis quinquefolia [on house already]			
Anemone, white (6) [gift]			
Atropa Belladonna [hedge]			
Auriculas [gift cuttings]			
Balsams (8) [gift seedlings]			
Bear's Breeches (*Acanthus longifolius*) [gift cuttings]			
Bergamot Mint (*Mentha citrata*) [gift cutting]			
Box bush (*Buxus*) [hedge]			
Buttercups [hedge]			
Camellia alba plena [nurseryman]	1	10	0
Camellia Lady de Saumerez [arboretum]		15	0
Carnations (*Dianthus Caryophyllus*) [nurseryman]		14	6
Chives [market]		1	6
Creeping Jenny [gift cutting]			
Crocus [in garden]			
Cyclamen neapolitanum (4) [nurseryman]		8	0
Datura Stramonium [seed from France]			
Dianthus Mrs. Sinkins (4) [nurseryman]		8	0
Dianthus Ashdown Forest [nurseryman]		2	0
Dianthus laced, from seed [nurseryman]		2	6
Euphorbia (2 varieties) [gift plants]			
c./fwd.	£4	1	6

	£	s.	d.
b./fwd.	£4	1	6
Fennel, from seed [nurseryman]			6
Ferns, English varieties [hedges]			
Ferns (*Onoclea germanica*) [nurseryman]		5	6
Fool's Parsley (*Aethusa*) [hedge]			
Foxgloves (*Digitalis*) [hedges]			
Fuchsias (2) [nurseryman]		9	0
Garlic (*Allium albopilosum*) [nurseryman]		4	0
Gentian [gift cutting]			
Geraniums (6 rooted slips) [Woolworths]		1	0
Geranium Crystal Palace Gem [nurseryman]		3	6
Geranium Distinction [nurseryman]		3	6
Geranium Trophee [nurseryman]		3	6
Geranium Golden Harry Hieover [gift cutting]			
Geraniums assorted [gift cuttings]			
Geranium Edith [nurseryman]		3	6
Geranium Groombridge [nurseryman]		3	6
Geranium Mrs. Green [nurseryman]		3	6
Giant Cow Parsnip (*Heracleum mantegazzianum*) (2) [nurseryman]		5	0
Gleditschia Delavayi [nurseryman]	2	14	0
Globe Artichoke (*Cynara Scolymus glauca*) [nurseryman]		3	6
c./fwd.	£9	5	0

29

		£	s.	d.
b./fwd.		9	5	0

Helleborus niger (Christmas Rose)
[nurseryman] — 5 6
Helleborus viridis [gift cutting]
Wood Sorrel (*O. acetosella rosea*)
Helleborus foetidus (seed) [nurseryman] — 1 6
Hollyhock (*Althea rosea*) [in garden]
Hop (*Humulus*), English [nurseryman] — 2 6
Hop, Golden (*Humulus Lupulus aureus*) [nurseryman] — 4 6
House Leek (*Sempervivum arachnoideum*) [nurseryman] — 2 0
House Leek (*Sempervivum arachnoideum*) (seedlings) [nurseryman] — 2 6
Hydrangea [gift cutting]
Inula helenium [nurseryman] — 2 0
Iris (Yellow Flag) [wood]
Ivy (*Hedera canariensis*) [gift cutting]
Ivy (5 other varieties) [churchyards]
Jasmine [in garden]
Lily of the Valley [in garden]
Loganberry [gift cutting]
London Pride (*Saxifraga umbrosa*) [gift cutting]
Macleaya cordata [gift cutting]
Metasequoia glyptostroboides [gift]
Mimulus [hedge]
Mint [in garden]
Onopordon Acanthium (4) [gift seedlings]
Paeonia obovata alba [nurseryman] — 8 6
Phalaris arundinacea picta [nurseryman] — 2 6
Plantain Lily or Funkia (*Hosta japonica undulata*) [gift cutting]
(*H. glauca*) [nurseryman]
(*H. lancifolia*) [nurseryman]
(*H. albo marginata*) [nurseryman] — 10 6
(*H. Sieboldiana*) [gift]
Ragwort [hedge]
Rosa longicuspis [gift]
Rosa omeiensis pteracantha [gift]
Rosa gallica versicolor [gift]
Rosebay (Willow herb) [hedge]
Shamrock [gift seeds]
Solomon's Seal [wood]
Succulent, variety unknown [gift]
Tradescantia virginiana [gift]
Tropaeolum speciosum (seeds) [nurseryman] — 2 6
Tulips, Parrot (30) [nurseryman] — 14 0
Viola Norah Leagh [nurseryman] — 2 6
Vine, Black Hamburg [nurseryman] — 1 15 0
Vine, variety unknown (2) [gift]
Wild Daffodils [wood]
Wild Strawberries [wood]
Winter Aconites (*Eranthis*) [gift]

c./fwd. £14 1 0

		£	s.	d.
b./fwd.		14	1	0

Wood Sorrel (*Oxalis acetosella*) [hedge]
Wood Sorrel (*O. acetosella rosea*) [nurseryman] — 1 6

TOTAL £14 2 6

£ s. d.

SCRAPPED AS UGLY
Apple Mint, Hollyhocks in quantity, Sages, Tarragon, Thistles (various), *Tiarella Wherryi* — 10 0

FAILURES
Some very fancy auriculas — 1 2 0
Fuchsia — 4 6
Geranium Mrs. Henry Cox — 4 6
Rose Roger Lamblin (Hybrid Perpetual) — 7 6

£1 18 6

ANNUALS
Ammobium alatum (seed) — 1 6
Ornamental gourds (seeds) — 2 6
Morning glory (*Ipomoea rubrocaerulea*) — 2 6
Kochias (seeds) — 2
Pansies (12 seedlings) — 1 0
Parsley — 2
Petunias, Suttons Empress (seeds) — 2 6
Petunias, Suttons Empress (seedlings) — 4 6

14 10

ORNAMENTS
Filter to make urn and bird bath — 4 6
Six wire hanging baskets in sale — 2 6
Large wire plant-stand in vestry — 5 0
Iron rods for arbour — 15 0

£1 7 0

FERTILIZERS, ETC.
Stable manure — 7 6
Sybol, Ant Doom, Cat pepper, Worm killer, Abol — 17 6
Raffia, old telephone cable, chicken wire, bamboos, Nippon, wire — 19 10
Grass seed — 12 6

£2 17 4

TOOLS
Shears, spade, fork, rake, roller (abandoned since), hoe, trug, small fork, scissors, knife (all free)
Mower — 2 0 0
Kneeling pad — 3 6
Syringe — 2 1 6
Flower pots — 5 0
Hose — 19 6
Seeding pots — 2 0
Sieve and grass rake — 10 0
Seed boxes from tea boxes (free)

£6 1 6

TOTAL COST OF GARDEN £27 11 8

A Country Garden in Norfolk

The path leading from the road to the front door. The grass floor seems to flow
continuously through the paving because of the wide grass joints. The
climbing plants on the wall of the house are kept down to first-floor level
for ease of trimming.

An entirely new garden layout for their small Georgian farm-house was
designed by Herbert Tayler and David Green, both of whom are architects. Only some of the existing planting was retained, namely fruit
trees, road hedges of hawthorn, two yews and a group of willows. The
whole 'floor' of the garden had to be replanned and new planting, paths
and drive were added.

The house stands between two orchards, encircled by farm meadows
with hawthorn hedges. Although a hedge runs right round the garden,
with only one view outwards to the meadow opposite, great care has
been taken to link the garden with its surroundings by keeping it in
character with them. There are, for instance, no very brilliant flowering
shrubs or trees, since these imports from abroad often look wrong in a

31

setting of green English landscape. The plants chosen, evergreens such as holly, *Viburnum Tinus* and privet, bulbs in many varieties, shrub roses and climbing roses (but not hybrid tea roses), berrying plants like pyracantha and cotoneaster; all these seem already a part of the English scene (even if by adoption) and their colours and branching habits are chosen to suit the existing orchard trees and willows. The floor of long grass underneath all these links the garden to the surrounding meadows. The character is that of a country garden, the main impression is of grass and trees.

The garden and orchards are now one continuous whole, linked by a single grass walk, eight feet wide, which runs round the whole perimeter, sometimes between lines of apple trees, sometimes across open lawn, and across the front of the house. The front garden now provides only footpath access from the road to the house and the drive has been moved to the back boundary, where it avoids splitting the ground area in two.

Because the site is level and there was therefore no interest of slopes or steps, the grass floor is treated as two contrasting textures, rough and smooth. The smooth areas are regularly mown and form wide walks, narrow paths or open areas of lawn. The unmown grass forms the majority, however, and in the long grass is planted a succession of suitable subjects to give flowers from spring to winter. It is cut once a year, at midsummer. The technique for maintaining the shape of these mown and unmown grass areas correctly is by small galvanized metal tubes driven well into the ground, leaving only about five inches showing, which are not noticeable in the fringes of the long grass, but show sufficiently to guide the mower. This makes it possible for some of the paths to be subtly curved instead of straight.

Where a more hard-wearing path is required, for instance round the house and its approaches, paving stones are used. These are all made of coloured concrete designed to weather exactly like real stone (whose cost would be excessive). These stones are set flush with the grass with wide grassed joints, or as separate stepping stones to avoid a violent geometric interruption of the spread-out grass floor. The architects' own specification for these stones is as follows: One part khaki 'Colorcrete', one part Portland cement, five parts coarse sharp sand. The slabs are two inches thick, of various sizes, and finished with a wood float finish. They are laid on a bed of sand, being either cast where they are

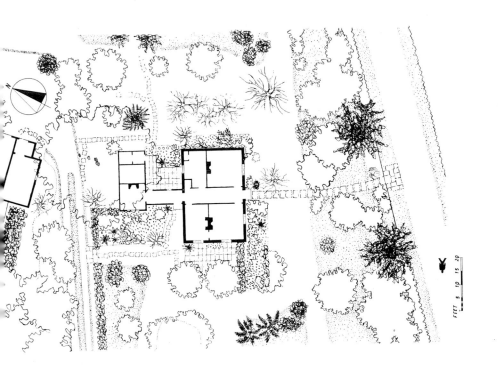

One of the garden paths leading to the garage. The trees are silver birch, crack willow and beech. There is a sweet bay-tree in the pot. The path is grass leading to paving stones nearer the garage.

33

The contrast between rough and smooth grass gradually increases from early spring to midsummer as the unmown grass grows in height. Starting with winter aconites, snowdrops and primroses in early spring, the bulbs continue in quantity and height until the May tulips, bluebells and varieties of white narcissus are out, as well as snowflakes, quamash, fritillaries and so on. The final and often most spectacular effect is the sea of common buttercups, ox-eye daisies, cow parsley and a few specially cultivated garden plants such as columbines, geranium varieties, *Iris sibirica* and *Campanula persicifolia*. Different grasses are also used. After the long grass is cut in June, there appear in September colonies of colchicum and autumn crocus varieties.

This tapestry hedge is of laurustinus, an old evergreen shrub full of pink flower buds in winter, becoming white in spring. Interplanted are two climbing roses, Albertine (pink) and Alberic Barbier (cream).

to be used or pre-cast and then bedded down. The important thing is the finish, if graceful weathering is to result.

The backbone of the garden is laid down in evergreens to give a restful winter landscape without flowers. After winter the three main effects are: spring – bulbs and fruit trees in blossom; summer – great shrub roses in the yard-high grass and in the evergreen hedges; autumn – berries of all kinds and the fruit trees. There are, of course, other plants outside this main scheme and the grass and meadow flowers. As most of the shrubs are set in the long grass, the earth bed necessary to their culture is unseen and the effect less harsh then when set into lawns. The stiff clay soil admirably suits both fruit and roses and the closely related berrying shrubs, which are mostly grown as individual specimens and not massed.

The existing road hedges of hawthorn have been kept, but new hedges, mostly enclosing the kitchen garden, are of evergreen flowering shrubs interplanted with climbing roses. They thus have three seasons; winter, when the evergreen foliage, shiny in the clean country air, is sufficient in itself; spring or autumn when the hedge plants are in flower; summer when the roses are out. The sight of the roses cushioned in evergreen leaves always causes astonishment. In fact, only strong climbers are culturally suited to this idea, but it is just such climbers which are normally so difficult to support, so rampant do they become without the root competition of the hedge plants. The historic name for such mixed hedges is most descriptive – a tapestry hedge.

MATERIALS
Paving Home-made concrete slabs.
Grass Floor Early spring – Primroses (*Primula vulgaris*), Snowdrops (*Galanthus*) and Winter Aconites (*Eranthis*); late spring – Bluebells (*Scilla nutans*), Fritillaries, Nar-

A paved area on the south-west of the house, shaded by plum and pear trees. The mown grass stretches out level with the paving into the orchard as an alternative sitting place. Shelter is given to this place by the house walls, a hedge of *Lonicera nitida* and the fruit trees. A glass screen is planned for the fourth side. Bedding plants in pots stand on the paving, while on the house walls grow a red China rose, *Clematis montana*, winter jasmine and, at the base of the wall, lavender, rosemary, cistus and megasea.

cissus, Quamash (*Camassia*), Snowflakes (*Leucojum*) and Tulips; summer – Buttercups (*Ranunculus*), *Campanula persicifolia*, Columbines (*Aquilegia*), Cow Parsley (*Heracleum villosum*), Geranium varieties, *Iris sibirica*, Ox-eye Daisies (*Chrysanthemum leucanthemum*); September – Autumn Crocus.

Tapestry Hedges *Berberis stenophylla* with white and yellow roses; *Escallonia Langleyensis* with pink and red rambler roses; Laurustinus (*Viburnum Tinus*) with climbing roses Albertine and Alberic Barbier; *Pyracantha Yunnanensis* with Penzance briar roses; *Veronica Traversii* with *Vitis quinquefolia*.

Trees near the house Beech (*Fagus sylvatica*); Birches – Silver (*Betula pubescens*) and Swedish (*B. dalecarlica*); *Cotoneaster frigida*; Crack Willow (*Salix fragilis*); Flowering Cherry (*Prunus serrulata Sargentii*); *Pinus Mughus*; *Pyrus salicifolia pendula*; Sweet Bay-tree (*Laurus nobilis*); Winter-flowering Cherry (*Prunus subhirtella autumnalis*); Yews (*Taxus baccata*).

Shrubs near the house *Ceanothus Burkwoodii*; *Clematis montana* and *Jackmanii* varieties; Cistus; Japanese Quince (*Chaenomeles japonica*); Lavender; Mock Orange Blossom (*Philadelphus Virginal*); *Pyracantha angustifolia*; Rosemary; *Senecio laxifolius*; Winter Jasmine (*Jasminum nudiflorum*).

Roses near the house Bourbon roses Kathleen Harrop and Zephyrine Drouhin; China roses, pink and red; Noisette rose Madame Alfred Carrière.

36

The entrance to this garden passes under a pergola and through a trellis, emphasizing that one is entering a deliberately enclosed space. Despite its smallness, all the elements which go to make a garden are present in well-balanced proportions.

All the different surfaces have a share in the design. The old wall of London stock bricks has been left uncluttered to reflect the play of sunlight through the leaves of the Blenheim apple tree round which the garden is shaped. The ugly wall facing west has been covered with a home-made squared trellis which provides support for clematis and other climbers, while the diamond-latticed trellis provides yet another pattern.

As the main object was to provide a sitting space, quite a large proportion of the floor surface had to be paved. This might have looked rather heavy if it had been done all in one material, so a small strip of

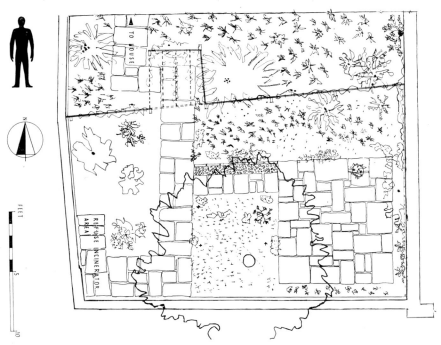

Pattern and foliage combine to transform an ugly wall.

cobbles was inset into the York paving. Such slight variations of materials, provided they are not so overdone as to be fussy, can help the design of a small area. It may be remembered that the designers of the Kon-Tiki raft made a special point of varying the materials used for different parts of the raft, and also the levels, to give themselves the illusion, in mid-ocean, of leaving one space and entering another.

The York paving was made from second-hand slabs bought from the local Borough Council for about £3 10s. 0d. (1956 price), a good deal less than the price of new. Many boroughs sell the stones which are taken up when the pavements are repaired, but some have a waiting list and limit each purchaser to two tons, which will cover about eighteen to twenty square yards. Many of the stones are broken and must be squared if rectangular paving is wanted. The squaring can be done with a heavy hammer and an ordinary cold chisel, but a special chisel called a bolster (costing a few shillings) is much better. The method is to draw lines on each side of the stone where the cut is to be made. When a few

Bluebells grow through a mat of wood sorrel under the apple tree.

incisions have been made with the bolster along the lines, the main part of the stone is held on something solid and the unwanted part broken off.

The stones, being worn, are of uneven thickness and must be laid on a soft dry bed – in this case the sifted ashes from the previous winter's fires. The first step in the actual laying is to excavate the area to be paved to a depth of about three inches, remembering that the final pavement should have a very slight fall in one direction to take off the water. A layer of ash should then be spread over the whole area, about two inches thick, so that the 'pavior' can easily scrape away material from beneath a thick stone or add more under a thin one. When all the stones are laid a mixture of cement and sand is forced into the gaps between them. For this, three parts of clean sand to one part of cement must be thoroughly mixed together and enough water added to produce a paste.

None of the planting needs much attention. A few shrubs, such as skimmia, forsythia, *Viburnum fragrans*, flowering currant and a small dark red feathery maple form a background for several varieties of iris, polyanthus and hypericum. Under the apple tree groups of bulbs and blue anemones are followed by bluebells, which in turn are succeeded by wood sorrel, a small self-seeding carpeting plant with a red flower.

The square trellis is made in sections so that it can be taken down when the wall has to be pointed. To give extra emphasis to the verticals, these were nailed on top of the horizontal bars, but from a practical standpoint it should have been the other way about. The vertical bars should be against the wall so that the rain runs straight down and does not rot the wood.

The garden was designed by an architect, Jeremy Dodd, for his parents.

MATERIALS
Paving Second-hand York stone; Cobbles.
Trees Blenheim Apple; Golden-leafed Elder (*Sambucus nigra foliis aureis*); Fig; Japanese Flowering Cherry (*Prunus Ukon*); Japanese Maple (*Acer palmatum sanguineum*).
Shrubs Buddleia; *Clematis flammula* and *pearl azure*; Flowering Currants (*Ribes sanguineum*); Forsythia; St. John's Wort (*Hypericum patulum*); Skimmia; *Viburnum fragrans*.
Miscellaneous *Anemone blanda* and *apulina*; Christmas Roses (*Helleborus niger*); *Cyclamen europaeum*; Gladioli; Iris; Polyanthus and groups of Hyacinths; Scilla; Wood Sorrel (*Oxalis deppei*).
Chairs Designed by Ernest Race.

The small scale of everything in the garden is magnified by its closeness to the living-room, and the shrubs and plants, viewed from indoors, are comparable in size with trees in the distant view.

As the situation of this roof garden is rural, a direct link with the surrounding countryside was desired. The living-room of the flat has good views down a wooded valley, and only a completely glazed wall separates indoor and outdoor living space. The garden is treated as a flat platform, partly paved and partly lawn. The small lawn acts as a foil to the countryside in colour and texture, and to the living-room in its formality. Small formal beds are planted with annuals and a fan-trained fruiting cherry has been planted against the white-painted wall for the decorative value of its flowers and leaves in spring and its fruits in the

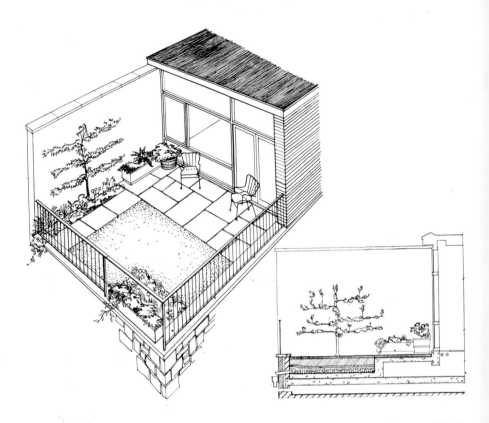

late summer. Two flower containers are kept on the roof, one filled with evergreens and heathers and the other with bedding-out seasonal flowers. One of these boxes occupies a focal point according to the season, as they are small enough to be easily interchanged.

The garden was built on top of an existing asphalt roof, already sufficiently strong to carry the additional weight without reinforcement. The roof was surrounded by a two-foot-high parapet wall and in order to obtain sufficient depth of soil the floor level of the living-room and the finished garden level were arranged at the top of this parapet. A layer of hard-core was spread over the asphalt, followed by a layer of fine boiler ash. To prevent excessive drainage under the lawn, inverted turves were placed next, and then the country loam. The final operation, after all had been lightly but firmly consolidated, was to lay the turves for the lawn.

The brick wall and the railings are painted in off-white oil paint.

The roof garden and the flat were designed as a whole by J. B. Blayney, a landscape architect, and John Sutcliffe, an architect.

42

For several years during and after the war this garden was derelict and overgrown with self-sown sycamores and elder. Its present owners, Professor J. Z. Young and his artist wife, found soon after they took it over that there was another drawback. About half the area had once been part of an old branch of the Regent's canal which fell into disuse and was filled up with bricks some years ago. The soil in this part of the garden is consequently only a few inches deep; nor is it very good in the remainder.

The Professor and his wife decided that it was hopeless to try and make a flower garden in such circumstances, especially as they saw that their neighbours, who had with great difficulty uprooted all the sycamores and elder, were unable to induce anything much to grow instead. It was therefore decided to accept the drawbacks and try to take positive advantage of them.

As it happens, the house itself proved a source of inspiration. It was built in the early years of the nineteenth century, when the English school of landscape gardening was still the fashion and houses were set in green lawns which swept straight up from parkland. Flower beds were then not much in evidence, partly because many of the plants which bring colour to the herbaceous border were still unknown in this country or had not been fully developed.

The Professor's idea of having a wild garden coming right up to the house was thus the right one artistically as well as practically. His task mainly consisted in removing such of the saplings and elder as he did not want and shaping the remainder in clumps, rather like the wings of a stage set, so that the drawing-room window looks down a green vista where light and shade are for ever changing as the sun moves round. One or two additional trees have been planted and some of the golden rod which had run riot has been shaped into groups. The garden slopes away from the house and there is a sharp drop of about four feet half-way down, to what was formerly the bed of the canal. A narrow terraced path has been made just above this point. At the foot of the retaining wall (which was the side of the old canal) a small sitting space has been paved with bricks which were lying about among the rubbish. The rest

Opposite: the garden sweeps up to the house.
Above left: from the drawing-room window, looking back to the broken column shown opposite.
Above right: established London planes are the pivot round which flow grass and sycamore saplings.

of the rubble was collected into a mound at one end of the retaining wall and sown with grass. A broken column found lying under a bush has been set up in the lower part of the garden and makes a convenient stand for candles when the summer evenings are warm enough for sitting out of doors. In spring, bulbs flower round its base and grow in the long grass near some of the bushes.

Dirty land that has lain derelict for a number of years will inevitably hold weed seeds in the soil. If time and patience would allow, the ideal way of cleaning would be to remove by hand all roots of the perennial weeds, such as docks, nettles and sorrel and allow the land to lie fallow for a season. As the weed seeds germinate in spring and early summer they should be hoed as they appear. Nettles are notoriously difficult to eradicate. Some water them when in full leaf with sodium chlorate. In this case the ground will be unusable for six months at least, but a year would be safer. There are also hormone sprays, which destroy weeds but leave the grass and soil undamaged.

This is a garden to be looked at rather than sat in, but it is just big enough to give its owners a feeling of contact with the soil and growing things. It was designed by Brenda Colvin and Sylvia Crowe, two landscape architects who found a prospect of bare brick walls depressing and who had the technical knowledge to triumph over the difficulties of making a garden in such a position.

Even in high summer the sun is on the garden for only two or three hours, so the first step was to whiten the walls with Snowcem in order to get as much reflected light as possible. Originally, the pots were on the zinc floor, but as this is really the roof of the basement below, the landlord asked for the pots to be raised off the ground, for fear their weight and dampness might damage the roof. This affected the design very considerably, and for the better, because once it had been decided to raise the level of the pots there was no reason why they should all be the same height from the ground and a much more interesting com-

Left: through the office window.

Above: from left to right the plants are: *Megasea cordifolia* (bottom left), Solomon's seal and petunias in front, with iris and a plume poppy behind. On the wall is a Virginia creeper, which is self-clinging on an ordinary brick wall but has to be pinned up on the Snowcem. Next come more iris and some columbines and evening primroses which re-sow themselves every year. There are bulbs in the same pots, which die down before the summer. The tree is a weeping cut-leaved birch.

Right: the first pot on the left contains a plantain lily, then come a group of royal ferns and a stag's horn sumach, which would do quite well in the sun, but even here it changes colour in the autumn.

47

position was arrived at. The brackets on which the pots stand are of slatted hardwood, like greenhouse staging, and were made to fit the garden by a builder, quite inexpensively.

One of the chief points to bear in mind about a pot garden is that it needs really a *lot* of watering, so there must be a good drain-away. It also needs more fertilizer than an ordinary garden. John Innes Compost No. 2 given once a month is the routine for this particular garden. Granulated peat added to the soil when re-potting has also proved helpful, because it holds the moisture. When permanent plants are first potted up, great care must be taken to make sure that the pots are sufficiently large to allow plenty of room for growth. Clean, broken crocks are placed over the holes and covered with small pieces of broken turf or other fibrous material, to prevent the soil from being gradually washed away through the holes.

The other important factor is the choice of suitable plants. Most of the plants here can do with very little sun, except for the iris, which are included for their leaves rather than the flowers. There are quite a lot of low pots between the large ones, with geraniums, creeping jenny and scyllas coming through 'mind-your-own-business'. The largest pot has ivy trailing down.

The names of the plants are given below. Others which could be grown here are *Campanula carpatica*, purple-leafed bugle (*Ajuga reptans purpurea*), hydrangeas and some of the smooth-leafed viburnums. A good alternative to the birch would be a maple, but it would be shorter and more compact.

The high walls give protection from frost in the winter and there is no need to surround the pots with sacking.

MATERIALS

Walls Snowcem.

Stands Greenhouse staging.

Plants Columbines (*Aquilegia*); Creeping Jenny; Evening Primroses (*Oenothera*); Geraniums; Iris; Ivy (*Hedera*); *Megasea cordifolia*; Mind-your-own-business; Plantain Lily or Funkia (*Hosta*); Plume Poppy (*Bocconia cordata*); Royal Ferns (*Osmunda regalis*); Scyllas; Solomon's Seal; Stag's Horn Sumach (*Rhus typhina*); Virginia Creeper (*Vitis Henryana*); Weeping Cut-leaf Birch (*Betula pendula dalecarlica*).

A Shrub Garden in Crawley New Town, Sussex

The most daunting thing about a garden in a new town or new housing estate is its utter lack of privacy, since most such gardens are partitioned off by chain-link fencing and have few trees or bushes. On the other hand the ground is sometimes rich virgin soil in which plants will grow rapidly once they have established themselves.

The tenant of this garden at Crawley, Mr. Sturk, is an engineer who is not a particularly enthusiastic gardener but who does like to spend his leisure in pleasant surroundings. He designed the garden from scratch with the same clear-headedness and precision as he would apply to solving a problem at work.

His chief needs, he decided, were seclusion, ease of maintenance, somewhere to sit and enough space for his sons to indulge in some, at least, of the unpredictable occupations with which boys of twelve and fourteen fill up odd moments, such as bowling imaginary leg-breaks and practising handstands. For the latter purpose a certain degree of indestructibility would be an advantage.

The answer to all this was found to be the planting of shrubs and shrub roses, allied to an interesting but simple layout. As will be seen from the photographs, the shrubs are already high enough to give some privacy, helped by the large tree in the neighbouring garden. The shrubs need very little attention, apart from feeding them about twice a year, and some of the roses, such as the dark red Frensham, flower the entire summer, so that there is plenty of colour and scent. Their resilience against tennis balls and the like is fairly high.

The curved planting line on one side of the garden and the path from the opposite side branching inwards in a series of right-angle turns have the effect of making the shape of the garden change as one walks about. It would have been a great deal less effective if both sides had been angular.

One unexpected thing is the secret garden, hidden from its own house as well as from neighbours. It is meant for sun-bathing but it also gives the whole garden a touch of mystery, such as was considered an essential part of historic garden design.

The sitting space, just outside the living-room windows, is paved and

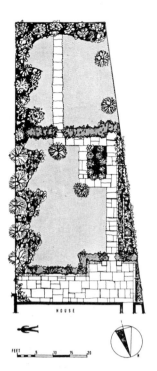

Above: the feeling of the Sussex landscape has been brought into this garden and in so doing the constraint imposed by the chain-link fencing has been triumphantly blotted out. The bold but fluid planting, unusually large for so small a garden, succeeds in giving added depth and a sense of freedom. The secret garden can just be glimpsed through the untrimmed hedge of cotoneaster.

Left: inside the secret garden. It will be noticed that, instead of the paved path, the plan shows stepping-stones, which might have been preferable.

Right: the sitting-space outside the drawing-room.

is separated from the main part of the garden by a low hedge of free-growing berberis contained within a low wall. The paved area is sufficiently ample to allow room for the family's activities when the grass is wet.

This is the ideal lazy garden for a busy man, since virtually all that Mr. Sturk has to do is to cut the grass.

MATERIALS

Paving Rectangular York stone.

Trees Apples (standard and espalier); Bay; Fig; Pears; Rowan (*Sorbus Aucuparia*); Thorn (*Crataegus*).

Shrubs *Berberis stenophylla, B. Darwinii pendula* (for low hedge); Broom (*Cytisus albus* and *Burkwoodii*); *Buddleia Davidii*; *Cotoneaster ambigua, Dielsiana* and *Simonsii*; *Escallonia Donard Seedling* and *Iveyi*; *Magnolia grandiflora*; Mock Orange Blossom (*Philadelphus*); *Viburnum alternifolia*.

Roses *Rosa Hugonis*; Floribunda roses Frensham, Else Poulsen and Masquerade; *Rosa rugosa Roseraie de l'Hay*; *Rosa spinosissima Stanwell Perpetual*.

51

A Pocket Handkerchief Garden near Sloane Square, London

This very small town garden, no larger than a sitting-room (15 ft × 18 ft), demonstrates how the maximum use can be made of limited space by someone who loves plants and flowers.

When Miss Vivienne Kernot, a stage designer, first took possession she found that all the walls had been painted white, in the belief that white walls would appear to increase the size of the garden. With her experience of stage *décor* she holds the opposite view and is now busily 'planting out' the whiteness with flowering currants, foxgloves, ferns, mock orange and various clematis and roses.

As can be seen from the plan, the paving is taken into the two farther corners, which gives an apparent increase in size. Additional growing

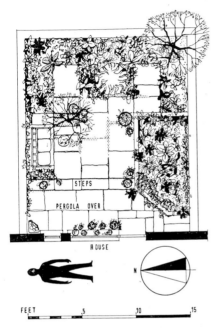

Left: the garden as an outdoor sitting-room.
Right: the pergola, with its trails of white *Clematis montana*, links the balcony to the garden. Its cross-bars have been bevelled off on the underside to throw off the rain. As can be seen here, wistarias, although hungry feeders, thrive in towns.

surface is given by the light-framed pergola which follows the shape of the paving just outside the house.

An almond and a laburnum take the eye above the walls and other permanent features are a paeony and a camellia which develop from year to year and whose foliage give shape to the garden. If, as so often happens, the design of a garden depends only on ephemeral plants, then all can be lost and the garden fall to pieces during a prolonged holiday or illness. Permanent planting, on the other hand, will stiffen and hold a garden together even though it may have to be neglected.

Much of the beauty of the permanent planting in this garden, which gives a constant background of green, is strengthened by the more

Above: from the kitchen door.
Left: richness without overcrowding.
Right: pots give extra growing space.

transitory charm of fuchsias, pelargoniums and petunias that are grown in pots placed on the steps and in strategic positions. In such a small space, too much strong colour would be dazzling and oppressive.

Valuable advice on roses, including the names of varieties which do well in towns, may be had from the National Rose Society (page 127).

MATERIALS
Paving Rectangular York stone.
Trees Almond (*Prunus communis*); Laburnum.
Shrubs *Camellia japonica Chandleri elegans*; *Clematis montana* and *Ville de Lyon*; Flowering Currants (*Ribes sanguineum* and *atrosanguineum*); Irish Ivy (*Hedera hibernica*); Mock Orange Blossom (*Philadelphus*); Vine (var. *Brant*); *Wistaria sinensis.*
Roses Climbing roses *Allan Chandler*, *Dr. van Fleet* (very successful), *Mermaid*; Rambler rose *Alberic Barbier.*
Herbaceous perennials Ferns; Foxgloves (*Digitalis*); Iris (purple flags); Paeony (*Lady Alexandra Duff*); Primulas.

A Danish Garden with an Abstract Design

Eywin Langkilde, the young Danish landscape architect who designed this garden for himself, would have liked a piece of modern sculpture as its main feature. Since he was unable to find anything that he both liked and could afford, he decided to substitute an abstract design of granite cubes set in the grass.

This is really a modern version of an old idea. For hundreds of years gardeners have from time to time made patterns of box and gravel, sometimes neatly geometric as in the Dutch garden at Hampton Court, sometimes in great twirling scrolls as at Versailles. The effect is rather like a rug or carpet, with its pattern varying according to the taste of the day. It is particularly effective seen from the upper windows of the house – a major point in the design of small gardens.

Mr. Langkilde's version has the advantage of being extremely practical, since it needs very little attention and leaves the whole of the space for his small son to play with his friends. It also sets off the free shapes of the trees and bamboos which are the other important element.

Formal flower beds in this kind of garden would be out of place, but there are a few shrubby perennials, such as single white paeonies, while the long grass round the edges makes a perfect setting for the specimens of wild orchis which Mr. Langkilde collects.

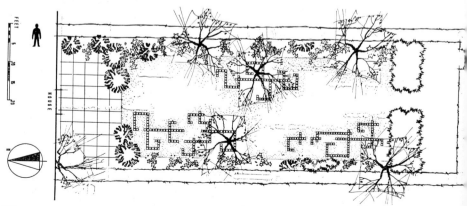

Above: the clean-stemmed trees
are kept in scale with the size of the
garden.

Right: from the bedroom windows
the geometric pattern is softened
by the feathery shoots of the
bamboo and the decorative foliage
of the sumach. The vivid autumn
reds and yellows of the sumach are
the only strong colours in this garden.

Rock plants have a particular charm for many people, but rock gardens as such tend to look out of place, particularly in an urban setting. They are difficult to make successfully and are notoriously difficult to maintain. A scree garden can be a pleasant alternative, where alpines flourish and can be seen to great advantage growing amongst the quartzite chippings.

John Ingleby, a landscape architect, decided to reconstruct an overgrown sloping retaining wall in his garden, and to build a new wall to retain a scree garden. A 'dry' stone construction was chosen, with the back joints mortared to prevent the penetration of weed roots. The garden itself was made by excavating to a depth of three feet six inches, below which the sandy sub-soil gave good drainage. An eighteen-inch layer of brickbats and stones was then bedded into a mixture of two-thirds peat and one-third sandy loam, to ensure a moist yet freely drained foundation. Above this layer was placed an eighteen-inch mixture of loam, peat and half-inch quartzite chippings. The surface was covered with an inch of quartzite chippings into which the roughly squared paving stones were laid to pattern the scree and serve as stepping stones. At one end of the scree garden a three-inch open-jointed drain pipe carries the rain water from part of the house roof, under the path and into the brickbat layer.

A few plants well suited to a scree garden are listed below but there are, of course, many others:

Arenaria	*Erigeron mucronatus*	*Oenothera riparia*
Armeria	*Erinus alpinus*	*Phlox subulata*
Asperula	*Frankenia thymifolia*	*Raoulia*
Aubrietia	*Gazania splendens*	*Salix retusa*
Campanula muralis	*Gentiana acaulis*	*Saponaria ocymoides*
Campanula pusilla	*Helianthemum*	*Saxifraga*
Cheiranthus linifolius	*Helichrysum marginatum*	*Scabiosa parnassii*
Cheiranthus mutabilis	*Hypericum Coris*	*Sedum*
Crassula sarcocaulis	*Hypericum olympicum*	*Sempervivum*
Dianthus caesius	*Iberis*	*Silene acaulis*
Draba brunifolia	*Leontopodium alpinum*	*Thymus*
Dryas octopetala	*Linaria alpina*	

Many London terrace houses have very long, narrow gardens which are difficult to lay out. The two examples illustrated are in the same Georgian terrace and were designed by their architect-owners. Both gardens are dominated by the brick walls and the views across them of the trees in the other gardens of the terrace. Otherwise they have little in common and show how designers with different points of view, catering for different needs, can produce completely dissimilar results from almost identical plots.

The first garden was designed by Frederick Gibberd for his own family. It is asymmetrical and is broken up into a series of compartments linked by a broad path which crosses to the opposite side of the garden after about a third of its length. The garden is thus never visible as a whole, but unfolds itself gradually.

The layout was determined by two simple needs; sitting space for adults and play space for very small children. Use by the children meant that there must be hard paths for the full length of the garden for tricycles and the like and that any exotic form such as a lily garden was out of the question. For the adults a large paved terrace was put down at the end of the garden which gets the afternoon sun.

The uncompromising character of the parallel brick walls and the absence of features between them meant that an informal layout would have looked forced. It was therefore decided to accept the geometric

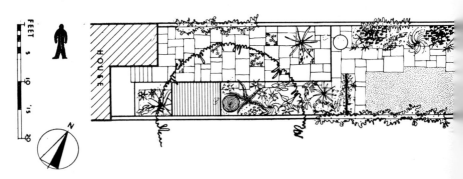

character of the plot and to subdivide it into a series of rectangles of differing proportions and character. Various kinds of hedges and screens separate these compartments from one another and help to counteract the strong perspective of the parallel walls.

The area nearest to the house is largely paved, partly because it is shaded by a large hawthorn and partly because of the comings and goings from the house doors. The pavings are a rectangular pattern of Purbeck stone with occasional insets of pebbles and the whole area is sunk below the general garden level to make it more interesting. The garden wall on the north side was whitewashed to give reflected light and a fig placed against it. The small garden on the opposite side, being in the shade, was planted for leaf shape and texture – iris, auricula, aralia and ferns.

The step-up from this terrace leads to the lawn section; a small bamboo fence with clematis and a vase mark the transition. A stone path separates the lawn from a flower bed against the north wall. As can be seen on the plan, this path was laid with rectangular slabs with the line broken on the grass side. The bed is not wide enough for a herbaceous border but is planted with hardy annuals, interspersed with evergreens for winter form. The garden wall behind this bed was made higher by a trellis covered with roses. At the end of this section grass is planted on both sides of the path to emphasize the width and the eye is prevented from penetrating further by staggered screens of privet and a stone wall surmounted by a timber trellis.

The path then crosses to the other side of the garden by a rectangular patch of random York stone.

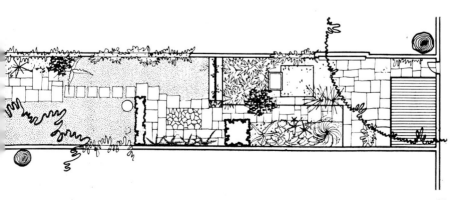

Left: Looking down the garden from the house. The magnificent established trees are given their full value.

Above: The screens from the side walls are staggered instead of being opposite each other, so that the path leads on more invitingly.

Left: a composition in white and green, sunlight and shadow.
Right: a variation in wall treatment.

The final rectangle is of stone and gravel with a sand-pit and stone sink for the children, associated with flowering shrubs like veronica, rosemary, deutzia and jasmine, and bold-leafed plants such as rhubarb. The terrace and summer house for the adults is next to this area so that a watchful eye can be kept on the children. To give colour, a white-painted recess for pot plants was made in the garden wall.

MATERIALS
Paving Rectangular Purbeck stone; random York stone; pebbles.
Screening Bamboo canes.
Trees Cherry; Dwarf Japanese Maple; Fig (Brown Turkey); Hawthorn; Sycamore.
Shrubs Deutzia; Jasmine (*Jasminum officinale*); *Polygonum baldschuanicum*; Privet (*Ligustrum ovalifolium*); Rosemary (*Rosmarinus officinalis*); Veronica; Virginia Creeper (*Vitis quinquefolia*).
Plants Aralia; Auriculas; Climbing roses; Ferns; Hollyhocks; Iris; Plantain Lily or Funkia (*Hosta*).

The Long Narrow Garden: Two London examples. No. 2

The whole of the second garden is in fact visible from the house, but the meeting branches of a fig tree and an ash form a leafy tunnel which hides the farther end in shadow and creates a sense of mystery. On either side of the central axis the flower beds recede by degrees and finally disappear altogether. In consequence, the garden appears to broaden as it gets farther from the house and the boundaries become invisible.

Within this framework the garden has been arranged to provide sitting space in both sun and shade and as many flowers as can be looked after without outside help. Breaking up the garden into different sections for different uses has also helped to disguise its length, despite the long stretch of grass, which was planned as a kind of philosopher's walk.

The doors from the house open onto a small paved area, useful as a drying yard and as an extension to the house for summer parties. Most of the wall surface is planted out with climbing roses (Mermaid and Albertine) and two clematis (Nelly Moser and Beauty of Richmond), chosen because neither of them needs cutting right back each year. There are, however, varieties which do need cutting back and it is well to be sure, for this and other reasons, that the right varieties are ordered for the conditions in which they are required to grow. This applies to many other plants and anyone who is unable to get the necessary information from books in the local library will find the catalogues issued by some of the leading firms of nurserymen most helpful in their cultural advice. A brief list is printed on page 128.

Plants in pots stand about casually on the paving, notably two fuchsias, both of which can survive a winter out of doors if the pot is covered with straw and sacking or partly sunk in the earth. Narrow beds link this section of the garden with the next, the north one planted with bulbs and bluebells, followed by nasturtiums. The south bed, which gets no sun at all, is given over to Tibetan balsam, grown from seeds imported from Hampstead Heath. Its only drawback is that it seeds itself up the garden so that a major weeding operation has to be undertaken each spring.

A path of York stone separates the two wide flower beds. Fortunately, there are no tall trees near the house, so it was possible to have her-

The pale pink double paeony planted near
the front of the border can be enjoyed
in its full beauty.

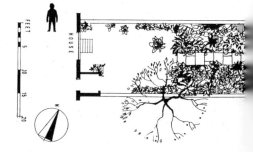

baceous borders where they can be seen and enjoyed from the windows. They have been planned to need a minimum of upkeep and rely on a few strong accents, such as paeonies and iris, which retain their form after they have finished flowering. Near the front, tufts of low perennials like yellow alyssum, aubrietia and dwarf anchusa with a forget-me-not flower (*Anchusa myosotidiflora*) break the line of the path, with gaps between for bulbs and annuals. Maximum use is made of the space by combining plants with different flowering seasons. *Lilium regale* flowers in the lee of the *Megasea cordifolia*. Early anemones and primulas planted in front of the paeonies and poppies have finished flowering before the leaves of the bigger plants are high enough to cut off the light, by which time the small plants are in need of shade. Many such combinations are possible, but this close planting makes heavy demands on the soil and calls for extra feeding.

Where the path meets the grass the beds narrow abruptly, making a flower-enclosed space for sun-bathing. The planting is simple and labour-saving, with alternate groups of old roses and iris and one or two paeonies for variety. It has the great merit of almost indefinitely keeping its shape unaided – an important consideration in planning a garden.

On the south side of this section a pear and a winter-flowering cherry have been planted to interrupt the view of the garage next door. These, too, prevent the planting from becoming dull.

Beyond the tunnel made by the two big trees is a green parlour where one can sit in shade and complete seclusion. It has been treated as a wild garden horticulturally. To increase the width, the grass grows right up to the walls, one of which has a high wattle screen in front for greater privacy. The walls are covered with honeysuckle, different kinds of ivy and clematis. Foxgloves, periwinkle, lily of the valley and southernwood

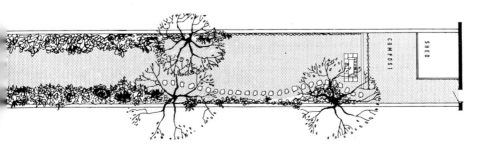

Above: the Tibetan balsam on the shady side of the garden near the house.
Right: under the sycamore tree at the end the planting curves out towards the
centre so as to soften the corner and half screen the continuation of the garden. It
was difficult to find a shrub which would stand up to the drips from the tree,
the dry soil beneath it and the draughts from under a door into the lane
at the back. The best answer was found to be *Olearia Hastii*, which gives form
in winter as well as summer and makes a good foil for naturalized daffodils
in spring time.
The trellis was designed to give a slightly horizontal effect to broaden the garden.
The length of the rectangles is one-third larger than the height. To the right
of the trellis *Polygonum baldschuanicum* on the side wall carries on the green
of the garden.

grow at the base of the wattle. A white-painted trellis, partly covered by a *Clematis montana*, has a wattle screen about a foot behind it, hiding the compost.

MATERIALS

Paving Rectangular York stone; York stepping-stones; concrete.

Screening Wattle hurdles; softwood for trellis.

Trees Ash; Fig; Pear (William's Bon Chrétien); Sycamore; Winter-flowering Cherry (*Prunus subhirtella autumnalis*).

Shrubs *Chaenomeles speciosa*; *Clematis Beauty of Richmond, macropetala, montana, Nelly Moser, and Ville de Lyon*; *Cotoneaster salicifolia floccosa*; *Fuchsia magellanica alba* and *magellanica gracilis*; Honeysuckle (Late Dutch); Ivies (*Hedera helix caenwoodiana* and *hibernica*); *Olearia Hastii*; *Polygonum baldschuanicum*; Winter Jasmine (*Jasminum nudiflorum*).

Roses Climbing roses Albertine, Etoile de Hollande, Mermaid, Ophelia, Shot Silk and Zephyrine Drouhin; *Rosa centifolia cristata*; *Rosa gallica Blush, Charles de Mills* and *versicolor*; *Rosa Moyesii*.

Herbaceous perennials *Achillea Gold Plate*; *Alyssum saxatile*; *Anchusa myosotidiflora*; Bluebells; Christmas Roses (*Helleborus niger*); Day Lilies (*Hemerocallis apricot*); Delphiniums; Erigeron; Foxgloves (*Digitalis*); Golden Rod (*Solidago*); Helenium; Hollyhocks; Iris; *Lilium regale*; Lily of the Valley; Lupins; *Megasea cordifolia*; Michaelmas Daisies; Ox-eye Daisies; *Paeonia Baron Schroder, Eva, officinalis* and *Rosy Dawn*; Phlox; Periwinkle (*Vinca minor*); Poppies (*Papaver orientalis, Marcus Perry* and *Perry's White*); Primulas; Southernwood; Tibetan Balsam; Trollius; Valerian (*Centranthus ruber atrococcineus*).

Seat Gordon Russell Ltd.

A Week-end Garden at Otham, Kent

The deliberate simplicity of this garden set in an orchard makes it ideal for a week-end house, or even for someone who frankly doesn't want to be bothered with a large cultivated garden, since it requires very little maintenance. Its architect owner, Brian Peake, designed the house and garden as one entity and made the relationship between the house and the trees a dominant factor in the design as a whole.

The garden itself is an extension of the living space of the house. The sun terrace is paved with stone slabs, broken by two rectangles, one cobbled and one filled with low-growing thyme. A nearby apple tree shades the small lawn, whose smoothness contrasts agreeably with the long grass of the orchard and its winding mown paths.

Near the windows of the house, colour is provided by the pattern of hexagonal-shaped flower beds, some of them raised above the ground. These can be filled with bulbs or annuals, according to the time of year.

Opposite, above: the meadow comes right up to the house.
Below: the sunny terrace with its bright flowers is seen through the shade of the apple tree on the trim lawn.

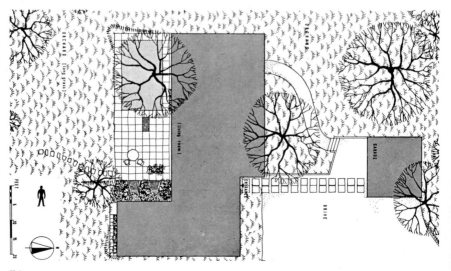

It would be difficult to find a less promising site for a secluded garden than this one – uneven ground covered with weeds, overlooked by neighbouring flats which provided a charming vista of fire-escapes. Only the most confirmed optimist could have hoped for the dignity and elegant simplicity which are shown in the subsequent photos.

Faced with the problem of creating beauty and seclusion out of this chaos, the owners very sensibly called in a landscape architect, Graham Lang. In addition to their general needs they asked him to provide a path from the house to the music studio, a sitting space, an area for a sand-pit and some screening from the block of flats. These requirements naturally affected the layout very considerably.

As so often happens, it is the designer's solutions to major difficulties which give the garden character; more, perhaps, than might have resulted from an easier site. In aiming at giving a feeling of spaciousness as well as a sense of enclosure, he has brought the lovely eighteenth-century

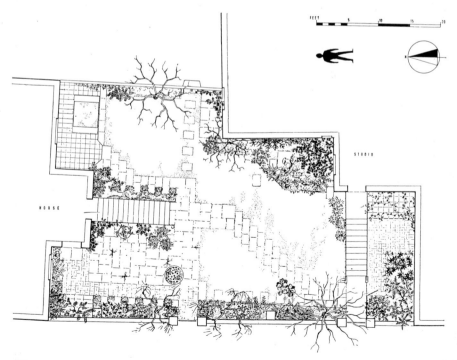

Above: the entrance to the garden from the garage drive, through the bamboo screen.
Below: the sunny sitting-space and stairs leading to the house. In the background is the newly-planted 25-ft high maple, which helps to screen the flats beyond.

Left: thick bamboo canes fill in the cavity under the stairs to the studio and make a background for the decorative leaves of a Fatshedera.
Right: the west side of the garden has been kept as simple as possible, to give a sense of spaciousness. The line of the original brick paving has been continued with stepping-stones across the grass to the flight of steps leading to the studio.

façade of the house into new prominence, with the garden as a foil rather than a challenge. The screening operations also make a major contribution to the interest of the garden. In front of a rather ugly concrete garage drive a framed bamboo screen, painted black and white, forms an architectural link between the house and the studio. It is mounted on a low brick retaining wall and the garden itself has been made up, with fresh soil, to the general level of the entrance drive. Approaching the gateway, the garden is half-glimpsed through the bamboos, heightening the sense of enclosure within the garden itself.

The framework of the screen could only be made by a skilled carpenter and might therefore prove rather expensive. If it is kept painted, however, it should have a long life. The bamboo canes, which are less durable, can easily be replaced. Their ends fit into grooves in the framework and when the cross-bars holding them in position (which also fit into grooves) have been taken out, individual canes can be gently bent and removed. It would also be possible to take out all the bamboos and use some other material for filling in the framework.

In front of the screen is a newly-planted maple tree, twenty-five feet high, which effectively screens the block of flats. It has survived transplanting successfully and its shadow is an important component in the design. People are sometimes tempted to move wild trees not much smaller than this one, but they are almost certainly doomed to fail. Nurserymen take care to move their trees each season, so as to break the taproot and encourage fibrous rooting – the reason why this maple cost as much as £25 to buy and transplant.

When the general level of the garden was raised it became necessary to have a trough at damp-course level under the wall of the house. This the designer used as an area for the sand-pit.

The centre of the garden is grassed over with fine grass and patterned with paving stones which form the two main paths. York stone was used and the size of the slabs was kept below a certain scale which related to the size of the garden. The apparently random arrangement of the slabs was most subtly worked out.

Most of the plants chosen need little maintenance and have interesting qualities of shape and texture, while tobacco plants (*nicotianas*) planted freely among some of the shrubs each year add evening scent and colour. The highlights are concentrated in groups of tubs on the paved sitting space, where agapanthus and bedding plants (mostly white, yellow and blue) give an exotic touch.

MATERIALS
Paving Rectangular York stone; brick.
Screening Bamboo canes in a softwood frame.
Trees Maples (*Acer*); Sumach (*Rhus*).
Shrubs Ceanothus; Clematis; Cotoneaster; Daphne; Euonymus (creeping variety); Fatshedera; Honeysuckle (*Lonicera*); Japanese Quince (*Chaenomeles japonica*); Magnolia; Mahonia; Rhododendron; Sarcococca; St. John's Wort (*Hypericum*); Vine.
Roses Climbing roses.
Herbaceous plants, etc. Agapanthus; Bleeding Heart (*Dicentra*); Bulbs (dwarf); Christmas Roses (*Helleborus niger*); Ferns; Iris; Japanese Anemones; Lilies; Narcissus; Paeonies; Plantain Lilies (*Hosta*); Scillas; Sedums; Tobacco Plants (*Nicotiana*).

Privacy and Communal Space in Holland Park, London

In many ways, this small garden in Kensington has the best of both worlds. A step through the wrought-iron gateway takes one into a communal garden that adds physical and visual space to the private garden. Town planners might well consider this a more convenient solution than the usual, but less friendly, communal square across the inevitable traffic road from the front door. For children there is a clear advantage, as they can come and go with safety through their own back gate, and private parties overflow informally into this peaceful oasis.

Mr. Derek Bridgwater has made his own garden appear larger by foregoing a high fence and by allowing the rich herbaceous planting to flow over into the outer garden. The traditional herbaceous border is usually banked up in a solid mass from the smallest plants in the front to the tallest at the back. Apart from the fact that this arrangement would have tended to cut off the view into the communal garden, there is a great deal to be said for allowing some of the smaller herbaceous plants to eddy through and around large plants or groups of plants. This method of planting not only has a less regimented air but gives full advantage to the shape and texture of the large plants that would otherwise be hidden.

Special expert attention was obtained by the tenants for pruning the forest-size trees in the communal garden, so as to let in the light and air

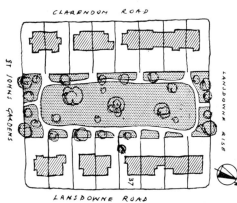

CLARENDON ROAD

ST JOHNS GARDENS

LANSDOWNE RISE

37

LANSDOWNE ROAD

Right above: the wise handling of the herbaceous planting disguises the boundary between the private and the communal garden. The scale is also happily related to the flowing lawns and forest trees beyond.

Right below: although there is a sense of spaciousness, brick walls on either side give privacy from the immediate neighbours.

Originally one end of the lawn was curved to leave room for a swing and sand-pit in either corner. Now that the family has grown up, the York paving has been continued to the wall to make a pleasant sitting-space. The staircase in the bottom left-hand corner leads to the first-floor sitting-room.

and to preserve the grace and beauty of each tree. The understanding care given to these trees is as refreshing as it is rare. A common mistake in lopping trees is to leave short snags or hat-pegs of branches projecting from the main trunk. Rot inevitably sets in which spreads into the trunk. A clean cut close to the main stem, pared with a sharp knife, will more quickly heal, and in the case of a major operation the wound should be dressed with a preservative. So often when trees are to be cut back to let in more light, branches are shortened, whereas they should be cut right out, otherwise a thick growth of small shoots will, in a short time, make the tree denser than before and ruin its shape.

78

This intimate and lively garden, designed by Mr. Laurence Scarfe, the mural painter and illustrator, has a simplicity that is almost classical, both in its colour and its layout.

The sitting area, which makes an extension to the dining-room, was dug out and the surplus soil carted away through the house, at no little expense. Mr. Scarfe's intention in putting the hand-made tiles on the low wall was to make the garden appear to recede, by the simple device of arresting the eye with the bold pattern and strong colours of black, red, green and white

The framework of the rest of the garden is dominated by a slight framed arbour that leads the eye through the shade of a vine to a reproduction of a classical head placed on a stone pier patterned with shells. The panel of wall behind the head and column is painted Pompeian red to throw the head into relief and echo one of the colours of the tiles. This somewhat unexpected colour in a garden goes very well, however, with the cream walls and the green of the hops and vine. White walls were tried at first, but found to be too brilliant.

This garden is unusual, perhaps, in having no grass; the whole of the central area is thick with flowers, mainly annuals, surrounding a stone urn.

The roots of the vine are planted in a stone trough against the cream wall, and the foliage conducted over the lightly built arbour. For initial economy, there is often a temptation to use rustic poles for an arbour

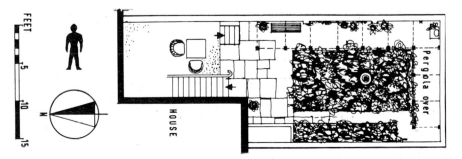

Above: the view of the garden from the dining-room window, showing the retaining wall decorated with coloured tiles designed by Peggy Angus. The boundary walls have been heightened by a simple but well-proportioned vertical trellis, in order to make the arbour more agreeable to walk under.

Left: an offering of ivy.

Right: the severity of the vertical trellis above the wall makes the diamond-latticed trellis seem less slight. Such variations in pattern in so small a garden must, as here, be used with discretion.

of this kind. These not only have a shorter life than cut wood which can be treated with preservative, but they would also be quite out of key in a garden of this character. Hop manure is used extensively on the main flower bed, but the vine is nourished on dried blood. Its sultana-like grapes are used by Mrs. Scarfe to make conserve and excellent wine. Between the pillars of the arbour are mop-headed box trees in green tubs, which not only add to the design but give out their delicious scent in sunny weather.

Mr. and Mrs. Scarfe's children have the great advantage of being able

The slender supports and cross-bars of the arbour give the vine plenty of room for free growth without taking too much ground and wall space. The column of hops growing between two piers throws a strong pattern of shadow on the wall. Decorative hops were planted at first, for the sake of the beauty of the leaves in late summer. Because they dropped their leaves at the end of August the common hop has been substituted, for this holds its leaves until well into October.

to play in the communal garden belonging to the square in which they live, but for more restrained activities they have a little house of their own in the garden.

MATERIALS
Arbour Softwood treated with creosote; the bottom ends are bedded in a pool of cement.
Walls Cream Snowcem.
Paving Large, irregular York slabs with cemented joints.
Tiles Made by Carters of Poole.
Plants Ferns; Hops (*Humulus lupulus*); Iris; Roses (Hybrid Teas); Vine.

A Highgate Garden

The plan of this garden echoes the plan of the house, partly because its architect owner, John Lacey, believes that such unseen relationships are subconsciously restful and satisfying. The arrangement also has the practical advantage of making the garden look larger; a remarkable sense of space has been achieved in what is really quite a small area.

Originally there was a broad path running straight down the middle with herbaceous borders, too narrow to be effective, on either side. Now the centre path and one border have been eliminated and the remaining border slightly enlarged, giving room for a broad lawn, whose width is emphasized by spacing out to striding distance the stepping stones down one side and bringing the grass right up to the border in between. On the wall opposite the border climbing roses have been planted. The new plan also solves the problem of the tool shed very unobtrusively.

The slight change of level at the end of the garden separates the terrace, which is mainly for grown-ups, from the rest of the garden which is used by the children, though they have their terrace too, leading out of their playroom-workshop. The planting on the grown-ups' terrace is small in scale so as to give an illusion of distance and increase the apparent size of the trees behind. The fountain, rescued from an old conservatory, is smaller than those generally used out of doors. Dwarf bamboos are planted in front of the end wall to give colour and form in winter as well as summer and in front of them are sweet-smelling plants – white only – such as tobacco. Large clumps of day-lilies and paeonies planted on the lawn soften the junction between wall and terrace.

The floor of the terrace is made of granite setts from an old building site, dry-laid over the foundations of the previous garden shed. This was a major operation, as the concrete foundations had to be pierced at intervals for drainage and then covered with three graded layers of rubble each about six inches deep, the coarsest at the bottom. Moss and rock plants are encouraged to grow between the cracks.

The upper terrace, gay with bedding plants in pots, has a lovely soft light when it is shaded by the striped blind.

Much of the beauty of this garden depends on the grass being well kept. Lawns in small gardens tend to get over-consolidated and hard

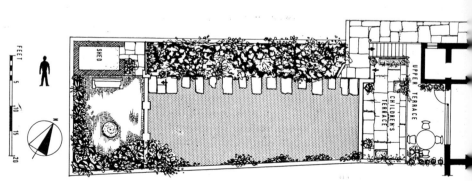

Opposite: from the upper terrace the garden spreads out like a carpet.
Above left: detail of dry-laid granite setts on the grown-ups' terrace.
Above right: Mr. Lacey admits that he deliberately planned a lazy man's garden.

through much use and continual traffic. As all plants need air at the roots for healthy growth a lawn can be much improved if trouble is taken to prick it all over in the autumn with a sharp fork, to a depth of about six inches. This somewhat laborious exercise should be followed by a dressing of fine bone-meal mixed in equal proportions with sharp sand sprinkled at the rate of four ounces to the square yard and swept in with a stiff broom or besom.

MATERIALS

Paving Rectangular York stone; granite setts; bricks.

Shrubs *Clematis Jackmanii, Madame Edouard André* and *montana*; Dwarf Bamboo (*Phyllostachys ruscifolia*); Fig; Ivy; *Polygonum baldschuanicum*; Virginia Creeper (*Vitis quinquefolia*).

Roses Climbing roses Etoile de Hollande, Madame Butterfly, Mermaid, Mrs. Sam McGredy, etc.

Herbaceous perennials Day Lilies (*Hemerocallis*); Paeonies and other border plants; Herbs.

85

A Housing Estate Garden in Vienna

The low wooden fence is a more human alternative to chain link fencing and accords well with a garden of this kind. The comfortable seat has good lines and can quickly be folded away. The sunflower, so often seen in Continental gardens, is easily grown from seed.

This garden was designed and laid out by the City Parks Department of Vienna as an example for new tenants on a recently built housing estate. It shows how the space can be designed for hard use and still remain attractive. There is, however, nothing in the garden which could not have been put there by the tenant, with the possible exception of the large natural paving stones of the path, but these could be replaced by spaced-out hand-made slabs such as those shown on page 31.

It is essentially a children's garden, since many young families live on the estate. The swing, sand-pit and small paddling pool are near the house, so that the mother can keep an eye on the smaller children. The sand-pit has a low raised wall, to keep the sand from spreading onto the rest of the paved area. The flower beds are also in this part of the garden, where they can be seen from the sitting space and give a background

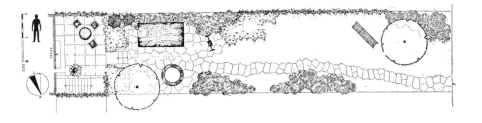

The trellis forms part of the design of all the houses in the terrace and provides a pleasant sitting-space, partially screened from the garden.

for the small children's play area. This leaves the rest of the garden free for the rougher games of the older children. Here, open planting of half-standard fruit trees and flowering shrubs gives the garden a furnished look and is fairly tough and resistant to damage. The path of rough natural stone does not run in a straight line but has a slight bend. It is laid about an inch lower than the grass, so that the lawn mower can be taken straight over it.

A birch planted near the house gives dappled shade without casting a deep shadow or taking light from the house as a denser type of tree would do.

The soil in the derelict garden behind the 1820 house was found to be exhausted with overwork and almost incapable of rejuvenation. To replace it with fresh country soil would have cost in the neighbourhood of £80, so the owner, Mr. Anthony Denney (photographer and collector), decided to limit the space for flowers and centre the design on water.

As can be seen from the plan, the garden falls into three parts. Below the steps leading from the house, the excellently arranged York paving surrounds a narrow rectangular pool, headed at each end with formalised stone lions. When this garden had been completed, the middle and larger section was tackled. Here again, a pool with the water flush with the brick paving is the centre of interest. Four stone columns are used to give height and to act as carriers for roses, honeysuckle and vines. The bricks for the paving were collected from the site during construction and are laid dry in groups of four to form a simple pattern. The roots of the large established apple tree had to be accommodated under the pool by shaping the bottom in such a way that they were not destroyed. An undulating bottom to a formal pool, necessitated by obstructions of one kind or another, is of little consequence since the water level will take the shape of the rim of the pool.

A feature of the middle garden is the bold planting of old-fashioned roses. This was a wise choice for, unlike the modern rose, they are very

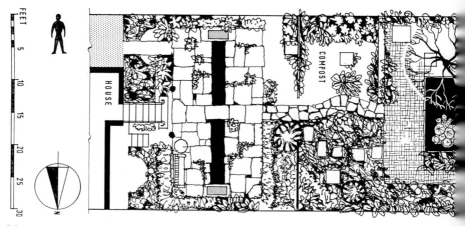

Above: steps from the house lead into the first water garden, which is seen at bottom left in the plan below.

FRUIT GARDEN

Above: the first water garden, before the second garden was completed. The squared trellis ran across the garden from wall to wall.

Left: the reflections of the white paeonies float in the pool like swans on a lake.

Above right: an unusual but highly successful experiment in mingling the formal with the informal.

90

hardy, vigorous, disease-free and, as can be seen in many deserted gardens, tolerant of neglect, since they need little pruning. Their scent is unrivalled and in a garden such as this one, where there are only muted tones of green, grey and white, the softness of their colouring suits their setting admirably. Some, like the rugosas, make attractive hedges and their second flowering period is followed by brilliant hips.

The last section, not yet completed, will be a vegetable and fruit garden.

The two pools have no drainage, but the water never becomes foul because a perfectly balanced community is kept between the oxygenating plants, fish and scavenging snails in a manner similar to a modern aquarium. A pool of 6 ft × 2 ft will need about twelve of these floating and submerged plants. The snails feed on the algae growths which cause the water to look green. The best variety is the ramshorn (*Planorbis corneus*) which, unlike some of the other snails, does not feed on the growing plants. Freshwater mussels are also good scavengers, as they filter the water through their valves and scavenge the bottom of the pool. Information on how to design and construct garden pools and the best aquatics and scavengers to buy may be had from the addresses given on page 127.

Mr. Denney finds that his garden is kept free of greenfly and pests by the birds which visit his pools for refreshment and stay to have a meal. On the whole, stray cats do not seem to like this garden because of its dampness.

There is a feeling of well-being and exuberance that is partly due to the continual moisture from the pools (replenished from time to time with a hosepipe), but also to the free use of well-decayed compost, that saviour of poor, over-used London soil.

Mr. T. Smyczynski, who made the garden, constructed the smaller pool (24 ft × 2 ft 4 in.) with concrete, covered with Pudlo, at a cost of £30. When he came to make the larger pool (41 ft × 12 ft), he found he could achieve a substantial economy by making the bottom of concrete and the sides of mortared bricks (1,200 bricks). The whole was covered with a thin layer (about half an inch) of cement compound mixed with waterproof Pudlo powder. The cost of this pool was around £35. Both pools are 3 ft deep.

MATERIALS

Paving Rectangular York stone; patterned brickwork.
Pools Concrete; bricks; Pudlo.
Screening Squared wooden trellis.
Trees Apple; *Catalpa bignoides*; Dwarf Juniper; Japanese Maple (*Acer*); Laburnum; Mexican Orange (*Choisya ternata*).
Shrubs, etc. Buddleia Colvilei; Californian Tree Poppy (*Romneya Coulteri*); Dwarf Bamboo (*Phyllostachys ruscifolia*); Forsythia; Hibiscus; Honeysuckle (*Lonicera*); Ivies (*Hedera*); Jasmine (*Jasminum officinale*); Lavender; *Magnolia Soulangiana*; *Polygonum baldschuanicum*; Rosemary (*Rosmarinus officinalis*); *Senecio Greyi*; Skimmia; *Solanum crispum*; *Sophora Davidii*; *Spiræa aruncus*; Veronica; *Viburnum Carlesii*; *Vitis Coignetiæ*.
Roses Climbing Rose Mermaid; species and old-fashioned roses in variety.
Pool plants Water Lilies (*Nymphea colossea* and *Gladstoniana*).
Herbaceous perennials Artemisia; *Iris Kæmpferi*; *Pæonia Duchesse de Nemours*; *Tradescantia Osprey*.
Miscellaneous Tobacco plants (*Nicotiana*); Raspberries.

A Vegetable and Fruit Garden at Crawley New Town, Sussex

All gardens look their best when they have matured and this one in a new town is in process of 'growing up'. As can be seen from the photographs, the architectural pattern is still somewhat strong in this unpretentious garden. The pleasure comes from being in a well-ordered and nicely arranged space. Vegetables, which can be so disorderly, have been successfully arranged in panels to provide an attractive frame for the social part of the garden.

The design is dominated by the curved wall of Sussex facing bricks – matching the house – and by the unusual and pleasing path. The path is laid on a bed of hardcore. The framework of bricks laid on edge is put in position and the joints mortared. The squares are then filled with a mixture made up of one part cement to three parts sand and six parts graded aggregate (the diameter of the largest stones being not more than three-quarters of an inch). While the concrete is still wet it is rubbed from side to side with the edge of a board which is long enough to be supported by the bricks at each side. This gives a ribbed surface which is safer to walk on than a smooth one, as there is less danger of slipping.

A low and thick hedge of *Lonicera nitida* divides the path from the lawn and serves as a backing and protection to the strawberry bed. *Lonicera nitida* grows swiftly and gives quick results, but if it is to be kept robust and neat it needs trimming three or four times a year. An alternative choice might be box (*Buxus sempervirens*), which, although a slower grower, only needs an annual clipping and scents the air on a summer day.

Where the path and the strawberry bed end, the lawn has an edging of mowing stones, which continues round the corner and across to the right-hand side. These stones are sunk an inch below the level of the lawn, so that the lawn mower can run along them, making it unnecessary to clip the edges by hand. An additional advantage is that plants overflowing from the beds rest on the stones, instead of damaging the lawn.

The square sitting space outside the house, seen in the bottom left-hand corner of the plan, is paved with large slabs of Horsham stone in cement. It is separated from the lawn by a yellow azalea and by a low

Above: the placing of the small tree is of considerable importance in the design of the garden as a whole. It is at its most effective when it is surrounded by smooth lawn, but the photograph was taken when the owners were on holiday.

Right: the brick and concrete path, flanked by the low hedge of *Lonicera nitida*. On the left, vegetables grow between the child's sand-pit and the brick frame containing the compost. They continue round the end of the lawn.

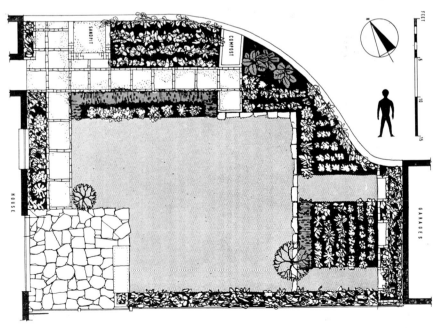

95

brick plinth or wall with a stone top, which makes a useful side-table for meals out of doors.

A belt of herbaceous planting, mainly of phlox, golden rod, ox-eye daisies, helenium and michaelmas daisies, hides the right-hand boundary from mid-summer on. It also gives colour to the garden, which until then has relied for interest chiefly on bulbs and the rambler roses and small herbaceous plants at the extreme end of the garden.

The orthodox way of producing apples from a small garden is to grow them as cordons or espaliers, and the curved wall (which at present has scarlet runners trained up it) would be an ideal position for them. Good accounts of how to train these trees are given in *The Fruit Garden Displayed* (see page 127). Another method is to grow dwarf trees produced by grafting onto a rootstock that limits the size of the tree. Many varieties can be grown as dwarf trees and a few are listed below. Both apples and pears can be grown as dwarf trees occupying six to eight feet square, but as there is no dwarfing rootstock for plums they must be allowed twice the space. The first requirement is a dwarfing rootstock and the second is planting a healthy tree. The surest way to avoid trouble is to buy trees from a good nurseryman. The Horticultural Adviser of the County Education Department will know reliable nurserymen and can also be consulted on other gardening problems.

With the apples, pears and plums which require cross-pollination so that they may set fruit, some of the difficulty of lack of space can be overcome by getting a neighbour to grow a different variety so as to ensure cross-pollination, possibly interchanging part of the crops. Any good fruit catalogue will mention which varieties require cross-pollination.

The following varieties of apples can be grown on dwarfing rootstock: *Dessert* – Fortune, Lady Sudely, Cox's Orange Pippin, Tydeman's Late Orange; *Cooking* – Arthur Turner, Rev. Wilks, Edward VII.

MATERIALS
Paving Horsham stone; Sussex facing bricks; concrete.
Trees and Shrubs Apple; Azalea; Cherry; *Lonicera nitida*.
Perennials Golden Rod (*Solidago*); Helenium; Michaelmas Daisies (*Aster*); Ox-eye Daisies; Phlox; Rambler roses; Strawberries.

From the sitting-space carved out of the ground near the house the greensward rolls up to the artificially created mound. The worn grey stone on the right serves as seat and decoration.

By virtue of its design this essentially restful garden needs little upkeep and is well suited to the lives of two busy architects, Mr. and Mrs. B. L. Adams, and their children.

The basic form was determined by the problem of disposing of *débris* from a large derelict greenhouse, and all the rubbish that had accumulated in a long-neglected garden. It was therefore decided to make a merit of necessity and consolidate all the rubbish, including the glass, to form an undulating mound, the contours of which are marked on the plan. The resulting three-foot-high mound has had the effect of making the garden look considerably larger and more interesting. The happily shaped slope, now beautifully covered with grass, drops down against the wall on the side away from the house to make the mound look more

97

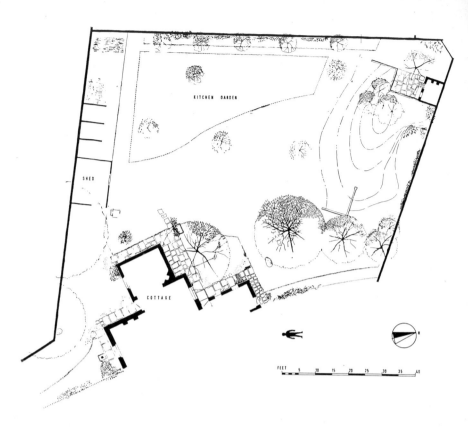

Left: through the fruit bushes to the house. The old laburnum, with its twisted trunk, has a statuesque quality.
Above: freewheeling down the slope of the mound.

natural, and incidentally gives a slight feeling of mystery much enjoyed by the children The thin planting of silver birches on its crest increases the importance of the mound. The whole garden is fortunate, too, in the shape of the established trees, which have been most carefully tended.

The basic lines of this simple garden are right because they are appropriate, and this is especially so of the charming line of the kitchen garden. Apart from the flowers for cutting, which grow among the vegetables and soft fruits in the manner of a cottage garden, there are virtually no other flowers, but as time and money allow, more planting will probably be contemplated.

The great aim in the making of this garden was to avoid spending money, and apart from the purchase of eight precast paving stones, some limes for pollarding and a few half-standard fruit trees, this has been achieved. The only maintenance expense is the man-power needed to mow the lawns and keep them looking gracious and well tended.

A problem familiar to the urban gardener, but unknown to those who live in the country, is how to lay hands on sufficient stakes and

A somewhat unusual but effective way of laying bricks to form a low retaining wall for the lawn and also a continuous seat round the sitting-space. Only the heads of the bricks are visible and they are dry-laid to provide congenial crevices for the odd rock plant. The head was carved by Theo Crosby from a granite kerb-stone.

100

Mr. and Mrs. Adams are fortunate in having an original pre-cast concrete figure by Theo Crosby, which has been placed with great effect on the high brick wall facing the front door.

canes to support the raspberries, the beans, the peas and the herbaceous plants. One solution which might find acceptance in a garden of this size would be to plant a thicket or hedge of bamboo. It is usually supposed that they need a moist situation, but in fact they succeed admirably on a poor soil, and even under trees. In addition to providing canes for the garden (and bows and arrows), they make an admirable screen and are in themselves most decorative. The evergreen bamboo (*Arundinaria japonica*) makes a dense, impenetrable thicket or hedge. Another alternative, in the absence of stakes, is to train the peas up chicken wire which can be used year after year.

The problems presented by this small rectangular garden of a modern terrace house in Kensington are typical of those which face hundreds of people living in new houses all over the country, particularly in the new towns. The chain-link fence which separates such gardens from their neighbours gives no privacy to the occupants and no protection to the plants. It seems only to emphasize the smallness of the plot and its rather boring shape.

Brenda Colvin, the landscape architect who designed this particular garden, has used a series of curves to break the rectangular shape and has placed the chief feature of the garden, a small pool, in the corner diagonally opposite the entrance to the garden from the house. This has the effect of leading the eye across the longest distance in the garden, which seems larger in consequence. To give privacy straight away, bamboo screens have been used near the house.

The family for whom the garden was designed wanted one which would be pleasant to sit in and to entertain in, but which would not need a lot of looking after. They also wanted space for a children's plot, so placed that it would not spoil the rest of the garden if it were neglected.

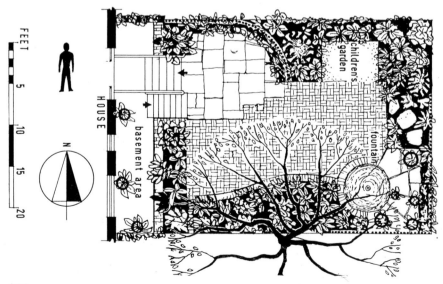

The diagonal vista from the house. When comparing this photograph with the plan it will be noticed that the garden ends just beyond the pool. The chain link fencing is successfully planted out and advantage taken of the beauty of the neighbouring gardens. The bamboo screen on the left is the further end of the curve which bends round the York paving. This can be clearly seen on the plan.

Within the curve of the bamboo screen on the side near the entrance from the house is the sitting space, paved with stone. Plants growing up the screen will soon give it a greater sense of intimacy. The curve also shuts off the view of the children's garden from the house.

A small step down and a change of floor covering from stone to brick marks the transition from the sitting space to the rest of the garden. Here the chief features are the pool and the raised platform behind it. The platform is paved with stone and acts as a stand for pots and tubs which can provide colour at short notice, for a party for example. This is the only point in the garden where bright colour is used. All the rest of the planting is subdued in tone, largely because it was thought more important to have permanent ground cover; and plants which give this do not, on the whole, provide large splashes of colour.

The pool has a small fountain and contains a few water plants, in-

103

cluding one small-growing water lily. There are small holes in the sides of the pool at intervals, just below the surface, through which water is sucked up by the plants nearby, making this area virtually a bog garden.

Most of the planting needs very little attention, except for pruning when it gets out of hand and an occasional dressing of compost or manure. There are, of course, places for planting bulbs and small plants.

One attractive feature for the housewife is the herb garden in front of the kitchen window.

The bamboo screens are made of natural unpainted canes threaded on wire, known as Riviera fencing. The size used here is five feet nine inches high and at the time of writing would have cost 72s. 6d. for a ten-yard roll, plus 10 per cent for immersion in preservative. Other sizes are also made. The fencing is mounted on a strong wooden frame, which involves a certain outlay, unless one happens to be a carpenter. It is as well to raise the bottom of the screen some few inches above the soil to prevent danger of rotting.

The bricks for the paving are laid in pairs to make a basket-work pattern. They are set in cement over a fine ash bed and the joints were filled in by brushing dry cement and sand over the surface and then spraying with water to set the cement, after each brick had been carefully freed from all trace of the mixture.

MATERIALS

Paving York stone; dark red bricks.

Screen Riviera fencing.

Trees Acacia; Apple (*Malus John Downie*).

Pool plants *Elodis canadensis*; *Nymphea James Brydon*; *Pontederia cordata*.

Shrubs *Amelanchier laevis*; Bay (*Laurus nobilis*); *Clematis alpina, balearica* and *Kermesina*; *Cotoneaster horizontalis, salicifolia floccosa* and *Simonsii*; Dutchman's Pipe (*Aristolochia Sipho*); *Escallonia Iveyi*; *Euonimus alata*; Fig; *Fuchsia Riccartonii*; Honeysuckle (*Lonicera*); *Hydrangea paniculata*; Irish Ivy (*Hedera hibernica*); Jasmine (*Jasminum officinale*); Lemon-scented Verbena (*Lippia citriodora*); *Magnolia denudata*; *Osmanthus Delavayi*; *Viburnum rhytidophyllum*; Virginia Creeper (*Vitis Henryana*); *Wistaria sinensis*.

Roses *Rosa Moyesii Nevada* and *Rosa spinosissima Stanwell Perpetual.*

Herbaceous perennials African Corn Flag (*Antholyza paniculata*); Bear's Breeches (*Acanthus latifolius*); Bugle (*Ajuga reptans purpurea*); *Campanula isophylla alba* and *muralis*; Cow Parsnip (*Heracleum giganteum*); *Helleborus corsicus*; *Iris pallida dalmatica*; Leadwort (*Ceratostigma Willmottianum*); *Lilium regale*; Lily of the Valley; *Megasea cordifolia*; *Paeonia officinalis, Duchesse de Nemours, General McMahon* and *Albert Crousse*; Plume Poppy (*Bocconia cordata*); *Primula pulverentula*; *Salvia officinalis purpurea*; *Saxifraga peltata*; Solomon's Seal; Herbs.

Ferns Royal Ferns (*Osmunda regalis*).

A Terrace Garden in Edinburgh

From Edinburgh comes a third and rather workmanlike layout of a long narrow garden, belonging to a Scottish architect, Alan Reiach, who designed it. The plan looks deceptively simple at first sight, but in fact everything has been very carefully worked out to fit nicely together without any fussy or clumsy corners.

Outside the house door is a terrace of paving stones interspersed with rock plants. Near the door, an overhanging wooden frame, soon to be covered with a Mermaid rose, encloses the view down the garden and through a trellis to a dark holly bush at the end, giving a sense of 'beyond' to an otherwise obvious space. Beneath the frame is the entrance to the drying yard, which is screened from the terrace by a well-built slatted trellis. Where there are small children this is a far more attractive solution of the washing problem than the familiar rows of perpetually flapping nappies.

The ground falls away very sharply near the house, so there is a big drop at the end of the terrace. The face of the retaining wall is gay with rock plants which were put into position as the building of the wall progressed. The stones were laid dry, each one sloping slightly backwards into the earth, so that moisture falling on the face trickles down

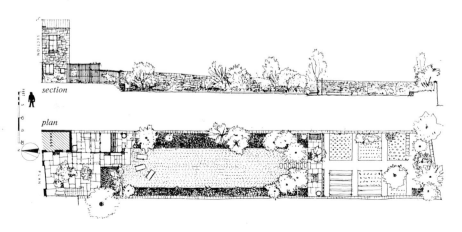

section

plan

Above: the entrance to the vegetable garden. The
position of the stepping-stones has been altered
since the plan was made.
Right: the terrace is planted with rock phlox, Spanish
gorse and 'snow in summer'. *Clematis montana*
climbs up the metal staircase and the decoration is
completed by a pot of *Rhododendron praecox*, which
is replaced by other plants in pots according to the
time of year.

to the roots of the plants. As it is impossible to feed plants in a dry wall it is important to see that the roots are planted in good soil and that the soil immediately behind the stones is also good.

The flower beds on either side of the lawn differ in width, so as to avoid too much symmetry. This arrangement also suits the side position of the house door, to which the steps from the terrace onto the lawn are related. The trees at the end of the lawn away from the house combine

Left: the raised terrace with its flowers softens the severity of the house.
Right: on the right of the flowered terrace can be seen the screen to the drying yard and the wooden projection which, when clad with roses, will encourage the eye to concentrate on the garden.

with the high stone walls to give privacy, and shelter from the notorious Edinburgh winds. Protection is completed by the flanking houses in the terrace.

A third of the garden is devoted to vegetables, separated from the rest by a slatted wooden trellis with scarlet runners and sweet peas climbing up it. The space in front of the trellis is treated as a separate unit, with an attractive block of plants linking a child's sand-pit with a small sitting space. Part of an old roll-top desk was used to make the seat.

MATERIALS

Paving Rectangular stone paving; stepping stones.

Screening Trellises of vertical wooden slats.

Trees Apples; Balsam Poplar (*Populus Tacamahaca balsamifera*); Elder; Holly (*Ilex aquifolium*); Laburnum; Lilac (*Syringa*); Rowan (*Sorbus Aucuparia*); Sycamore (*Acer pseudo-platanus*).

Shrubs Buddleia; *Clematis montana*; Flowering Currant (*Ribes sanguineum*); Ivy (*Hedera*); Lavender; Mock Orange Blossom (*Philadelphus*); *Rhododendron praecox*; Wistaria.

Terrace planting Catmint (*Nepeta*); Jerusalem Star (*Cerastium tomentosum*); Rock Phlox; Snow in summer (*Ozomanthus rosmarinifolius*); Spanish Gorse (*Genista hispanica*).

Miscellaneous Climbing rose Mermaid; Herbaceous perennials; Vegetables.

108

A Children's Garden in St. John's Wood, London

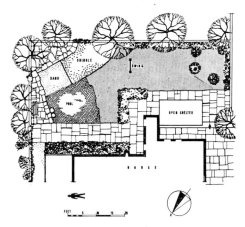

It is often a real difficulty in a small garden to find space for children to play without wholesale destruction of plants precious to adults. Children, in fact, are in danger of being tidied out of existence.

It is refreshing, therefore, to find a garden almost wholly devoted to the basic pleasures of young children. The elements of contented play are all found in this garden, designed by Brenda Colvin: sand, water, grass and delicious rounded pebbles that make an engrossing pattern under the water and are so exciting for small feet. It is unusual also, in a garden, to find water and sand so close together. Either is good to play with but together they re-create the pleasure of the seaside.

The pebble pool is filled by a hose and has a plug-hole for easy emptying. Near the sand compartment is a stretch of washed shingle – good for sun-bathing – on which will soon be placed a small dinghy to give added delight. The sand and the shingle are contained in their separate compartments by a narrow stone band.

Two boulders act as steps to the upper paved terrace, which has a seat under the shade of the trees. The brick wall is heightened by hand-made wattle hurdles framed in painted hardwood, upon which are trained jasmine and clematis.

Half-standard flowering cherries give dappled shade to the lawn be-

Above: the transition from pebble beach to lawn, with
the wistaria screen behind. Up the corner of the
screen climbs an everlasting pea, which does well
in London.
Right: chunky stones serve as steps or seat.

neath and this stretch of grass is useful also for hanging out the washing. Under the nursery window is a bed of mixed herbs and the open shelter is partially screened by a low, open fence carrying a swathe of wistaria.

MATERIALS

Paving Rectangular York stone.

Children's play area Cobbles set in cement; sand; shingle.

Screening Wattle hurdles.

Trees Japanese Flowering Cherries (*Prunus Tai Haku*).

Shrubs *Buddleia alternifolia*; *Clematis alpina* and *Spooneri*; *Cotoneaster horizontalis*; Dutchman's Pipe (*Aristolochia Sipho*); *Escallonia Donard Seedling*; Honeysuckle (*Lonicera japonica flexuosa*); Hydrangea; Ivies (*Hedera caenwoodiana* and *tricolor*); Mahonia; *Spiraea Anthony Waterer*; Virginia Creeper (*Vitis Henryana*); Wistaria.

Herbaceous perennials, etc. *Epimedium pinnatum*; Everlasting Pea (*Lathyrus latifolius*); Paeonies; *Sedum spectabile*; Tradescantia; Herbs.

111

An Informal Garden at Strand-on-the-Green

Interest in this informal and friendly garden centres largely on the planting. The plan is simple, helped by a slight rise in the ground away from the house, but the pleasantly arranged stepping stones and an old brick wall on one side give a basic sense of form.

The house is at the end of a terrace and the garden is separated from its neighbour by a chain-link fence. Along this are planted, at intervals, a small willow, some fruiting quinces, hybrid musk and climbing roses, also a rhododendron. These give light but adequate screening to the gardens on either side of the fence without marking the boundary line as rigidly as a hedge would do. The garden is close to the Thames so that the willow and the quinces, both of which need moisture, are particularly suitable. There are several varieties of willow which never grow higher than twelve to fifteen feet and are consequently suitable for planting near a house where screening is required. Among these are *Salix caprea pendula, incana, magnifica* and *purpurea*. A screen at the end of the garden is being grown from willow slips, which root with the greatest of ease.

Against the brick wall is a fan-trained peach. There is a narrow service path between the tree and the large flower bed.

The planting in the flower beds flanking the path is the same on both sides and consists largely of plants with foliage of an interesting shape or colour, which continue to be decorative when they have stopped flowering. These include: cotton lavender, Mrs. Sinkins pinks, lamb's ears and *Senecio Greyi* – all with grey leaves – various irises, *Anchusa myosotidiflora*, candytuft. One or two old-fashioned roses and a few shrubs such as *Diervilla praecox* and *Mahonia japonica* help to vary the height. The result is a pleasant impression of liveliness almost all the year round. Planting such as this needs very little maintenance. Other plants which could be used in such a scheme are: Rosemary, catmint (*Nepeta*), day lilies (*Hemerocallis*), globe thistle (*Echinops*), sea holly (*Eryngium*) and possibly mullein (*Verbascum*) or plume poppy (*Bocconia cordata*) for height. The garden gets quite a lot of sun, so that it would be unsuitable for some of the other plants with good foliage, such as plantain lilies (*Hosta*) or spiraea and astilbe, while larger plants, like gunnera, would

The billowing froth of the willow is echoed by the curve of the stepping-stones.

be out of scale with the rest of the garden.

In front of the dwarf box hedge at the end of the flower beds facing the house are alternate clumps of strawberries and winter-flowering heath (*Erica carnea*), to provide interest in both summer and winter.

113

The strong spears of the iris contrast well with the grey foliage of the pinks.

This is an instance of the importance of selecting the right variety of plant in a particular species. *Erica carnea* is one of the few heaths that tolerate lime, which is congenial to both box and strawberries.

MATERIALS

Paving Rectangular concrete slabs; York stepping stones; bricks.

Trees Double Almond (*Prunus communis roseo pleno*); Peach (*Royal George*); Willow (*Salix*).

Shrubs Box (*Buxus suffruticosa*); Cotton lavender (*Santolina Chamaecyparissus*); *Diervilla praecox*; *Mahonia japonica*; Quinces; Rhododendron; *Senecio Greyi.*

Roses Climbers, gallicas and hybrid musk.

Herbaceous perennials *Anchusa myosotidiflora*; Border Pinks (*Dianthus Mrs. Sinkins* and *William Brownhill*); Candytuft (*Iberis sempervirens*); Iris; Lamb's ears (*Stachys lanata*); Winter-flowering Heath (*Erica carnea*).

A Riverside Garden at Twickenham

There is a type of riverside garden which is quite unlike ordinary gardens in two important respects. It is separated from the house by a road and it has its centre of interest and sitting space at the furthest point away from the house, by the water. This is such a garden. Two further factors which played an important part in the design of this garden were its narrowness in relation to its length and the necessity for two marked changes of level, one at either end. It has been completely replanned and remade by its present owners, Neville Conder and his wife, both of whom are architects.

Their first act was to cut back by about two feet the privet hedge which, bulging out over the garden down the length of one side, made it look even narrower. As a result, the willow tree growing on the river bank can now be seen immediately one enters the garden, hinting at the presence of the unseen river beyond.

Partly from necessity and partly to break up its length, the garden has been divided into four sections. They are the entrance, the orchard, the flower garden and the river terrace. The gate from the road opens onto the rectangular entrance, paved with large pebbles set in cement. To the left are flowering shrubs, on the right steps lead down to the orchard. The paved area covers the massive foundations of an old garage, which it would have been almost impossible to remove. These have therefore been incorporated into the design and their hard outlines softened by shrubs and by some ivy planted at the base of one corner and trained up and along the side near the steps.

Just inside the orchard is a fairly high brick structure, hidden in foliage, which contains the compost. Its bulk helps to reduce the scale of the paved area and, by partially concealing the rest of the garden, makes it seem slightly mysterious.

The orchard consists of a row of five apple trees down the middle. To give extra width the grass is taken right up to the boundaries and between the stepping stones. There is plenty of room here for the two children to play, though in fact they range all over the garden.

After the pleasant simplicity of the orchard the garden becomes richer in interest. First come the flowers, concentrated in one big bed, with a

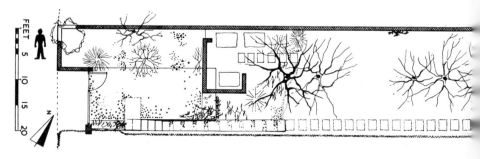

Opposite top: the concrete stepping-stones of the path have pebbled paving between them in the entrance garden and grass when they reach the orchard.
Opposite left centre: in a flower bed of this width, access to the plants should be made easy by gardening stones, which look better than patches of trodden-down earth. Here they have been arranged to make a pleasant pattern.
Opposite right centre: the orchard and the flower garden.
Above: the path beside the flower bed reverts to alternate concrete slabs and pebbles. The steps were taken from an old hearth and are very well proportioned. A general guide for making steps is that twice the height of the riser plus the depth of the tread should equal twenty-four inches.

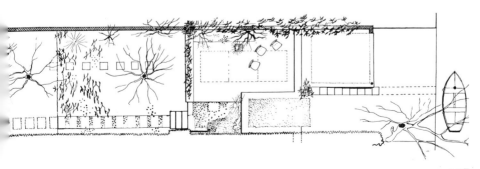

Above: the river terrace. The paving is of concrete slabs relieved by a discreet amount of crazy paving and a small square of pebbles.
Right: the willow beyond the camomile lawn on the right terminates the garden.

line of stepping stones for ease of gardening in damp soil. The whole garden is flooded on an average every other year, so that it is no good putting in plants which like dry conditions. There is also some shade from a sixth apple tree, but ordinary herbaceous plants like delphiniums, iris and helenium seem to do quite well and paeonies are most successful. Roses are not satisfactory. In general, plants which are described as needing good drainage have to be given a substratum of hardcore. Ferns brought from the country help to give ground covering.

Four steps lead up to the garden's high spot, the paved terrace where one can sit and watch the river. Seclusion from the road is made more complete by a widely spaced metal trellis (ex Festival of Britain) up which various climbing plants are being trained. The two-foot-high river wall round the terrace was originally turned inwards to allow for a boat-hard, which has since been filled in and covered with a camomile lawn, scented and soft to lie on in the sun. Camomile seed is not easy to procure, but it can generally be obtained from Suttons of Reading.

Making the river terrace was a tremendous task. It is built with the remains of the walls of the old garage, which had to be disposed of.

The concrete slabs for the terrace and the paths cost about £11. Reject

ballast from an aggregate supply company was used for the pebble paving, and cost about thirty shillings. The pebbles have to be set by hand in a layer of cement screed (one part cement to one part sand). This begins to dry quickly so that it is best to work in small sections. To make the pebbles stand out, the paving is hosed and brushed when the screed is almost dry. This may take anything from four hours in a heat wave to twenty-four hours in cold weather.

No outside labour was used in the construction of this garden.

MATERIALS
Paving Concrete slabs; reject ballast for pebble paving; crazy paving; hearthstones for steps.
Trees Apples; Willow.
Plants Shrubs and herbaceous perennials which tolerate moist conditions; Camomile.
Chairs Designed by Ernest Race.

119

Sculpture and Decoration

To some people, a garden is incomplete without a piece of sculpture or something of that nature. They may share Miss Barbara Jones's view that a garden should contain some object which is not alive and if, like her, they are content with a well-chosen piece of *nature morte*, they are among the lucky ones. They may, however, feel the need for some symbol of the art of man to counterbalance and contrast with the natural shapes of the plants. If their taste is for the classical, they can spend happy hours poking about in junk shops looking for something suitable that is not too expensive, such as the horse's head shown opposite. This fragment from the Parthenon frieze is reproduced in concrete from a mould made by an art student from a plaster cast. It is not sufficiently important to stand in an open position, but looks well among the grey-green foliage of Mr. Denney's garden. Another solution is an old ship's figurehead, and even an old wooden cart-wheel has a romantic air, particularly in an informal garden, such as Professor Young's.

The unlucky people are those who feel that their garden calls for a piece of contemporary sculpture, but who have only limited funds. Owing to the high cost of stone and bronze, even a small work by an established sculptor is likely to cost more than the average person feels able to spend on a piece of sculpture for the garden. Some sculptors have been experimenting with concrete, but unless it is specially treated it may eventually disintegrate, and in any case it often has a rather coarse texture which is discordant in a garden. In the high-relief 'Pink Horses', by Alwen Hughes, a student at the Royal College of Art, this gritty effect has been avoided by using a very fine aggregate and by adding a little colour during the process of casting. Reliefs are particularly suitable for very small gardens, since they can be set in the walls and need occupy no floor space.

Terracotta is another cheap material and if a fair amount of 'grog' (clay that has already been fired) is used in its composition and the figure itself is hollow, it will withstand frost and rain. It can also be treated with wax, or even with gold paint covered with boot polish.

Perhaps the most hopeful sources of supply are the art schools. Many schools hold annual exhibitions of students' work and others are glad

A concrete reproduction of a fragment from the Parthenon frieze (*top left*) is an interesting foil to plant forms. Old ships' figureheads (*top right*) serve a similar purpose. Rita Ling's *Orpheus* (*bottom left*) is an example of terracotta modelling. Alwen Hughes' *Pink Horses* (*bottom right*) is cast in concrete with a very fine aggregate.

to let visitors tour the studios from time to time. Here it may be possible to find, for a fair but relatively modest price, an original piece of sculpture. And even if the individual may not succeed and the immediate object of the visit is not realized, such contacts may be the means of bringing together the producer and the consumer, to the enlightenment

Some pots with character but without whimsy. An old wash-house copper and a Provençal vase (*top left*); an earthenware pot designed by Gordon Russell (*top right*) and one designed by George Wilkinson (*bottom left*); a hand-made Danish example designed by Herman A. Kähler.

and benefit of both.

There seems to be no tradition in this country for designing and making gracious garden pots. Now that they are being more extensively used and play so important a part in gardens and public parks it should not be necessary to turn to other countries.

A garden shelter, however lightly constructed, serves as a focal point and a pleasant setting for outdoor meals. The top one is designed by the Austrian landscape architect, Eduard Ihm; the lower by the German designer Otto Valentien.

123

Town soils are often thought to be used up and impoverished when in fact they may simply be in need of attention. The soot and other impurities that fall will quickly stifle the soil unless the surface is kept constantly hoed. This not only prevents caking but helps the rains to dissolve and wash away the acid deposits.

It is important to discover whether the soil is over-acid and in need of lime before planting is begun. Not everyone realizes that soil fertility is dependent on the presence of living bacteria and that these indispensable agents cannot live and do their work in a soil that is *unduly* acid or waterlogged. The majority of plants thrive best in a soil that is slightly though not over-acid and this is especially true of grass. Some plants, however, such as the camellias, azaleas, some of the rhododendrons, and lilies that do well in a smoky atmosphere, are lime haters. If in doubt about the degree of acidity of the soil, a wise step is to analyse the soil oneself by purchasing for the purpose a kit that is sold at most stores. This check will, however, only provide a rough estimate. A more accurate analysis can be obtained either with the help of a local chemist, or by sending samples to the County Horticultural Adviser, who will also, incidentally, be willing to give other advice on gardening problems. Samples should be taken from different parts of the garden, mixed together and a small quantity taken from the whole. A liberal dressing of garden lime spread on the surface of the soil in the autumn will wash through the soil during the winter and help to counteract undue acidity.

Many soils, especially in towns, are often starved of decayed organic matter or humus which helps to retain moisture and provides a good rooting medium. Farm-yard manure, one form of humus, is expensive and often difficult to obtain, but every garden will produce sufficient waste vegetable matter that can be turned into fine manure if trouble is taken to compost it.

It is of little use simply to pile up in an odd corner all the dead and living *débris* and hope for the best. It is even worse to stuff the rubbish into a concrete or corrugated iron box without ventilation. The rotting-down process is achieved by micro-organisms and these die if they are denied air or if the heap becomes waterlogged. They thrive best and

A luxuriant garden, fed on compost, in St. John's Wood.

work hard in a warm, damp atmosphere. A container, about two to three feet square, can be made of wood slats, wire mesh, or loose brick with ventilation holes, and should have a base of rubble for drainage and some protection from heavy rain.

The perfectionist compost-maker will only use fresh material and will exclude anything that has lost its vitality, such as dead leaves and the cooked remains from the kitchen, or even wilted plants. On the other hand, there are those who put almost everything onto the heap, including torn-up newspapers. The total harvest of weeds, lawn mowings and grubbed up annuals should be chopped with a sharp spade to allow the juices to flow and to ensure admixture of textures. The layers are spread evenly, lightly firmed, and given a sprinkling of soil and lime. Any manure, such as poultry droppings, will enrich the pile and an old sack over the top will help conserve the heat. A heap made in this fashion will rot down well, but it can be hastened by using an activator. Many types are sold but it is now thought that some of the chemical activators, although they work fast, destroy the micro-organisms, whereas herbal activators stimulate their work.

The ideal is to have three heaps. The spring and summer collection should be ready for use in about six weeks; the autumn one rather longer; and the winter pile will not be ready until the following spring. Most gardens are, however, too small to allow so much space. In this case two piles should serve. The spring and summer compost should be ready for use in the autumn and the autumn and winter pile should be ready in late spring.

Compost should never be buried more than four inches in the soil and is best used as a mulch round special plants.

An additional form of organic manure may be had from some progressive sewage disposal works. This highly concentrated fertilizer, which has been specially treated, is easy to handle and has no unpleasant smell. Other useful forms of feeding are bone-meal (in various grades of coarseness), dried blood and National Growmore fertilizer. Hop manure and peat will be found useful as a mulch to prevent the soil drying out and to add a fibrous content to the soil.

This book deliberately does not attempt to give detailed information on the selection of plants and their culture because there are so many excellent books on specialist subjects that can easily be consulted. Incidental sources of information have, however, been discovered by the authors, and these may prove helpful to others. It is not claimed that the following notes are by any means exhaustive.

THE INSTITUTE OF LANDSCAPE ARCHITECTS, 2 Guilford Place, W.C.1, will supply names of professional landscape architects willing to give advice on lay-out, design and planting.

THE ROYAL HORTICULTURAL SOCIETY, Vincent Square, London, S.W.1, offers valuable advice to members for a minimum subscription of two guineas a year. In addition to the use of the library and free entrance to the fortnightly shows at Vincent Square and to the Chelsea Flower Show, this service includes:

Naming of fruits (1s. charged for each sample named), general examination of soil, with recommendations for treatment (10s. per sample) and naming of plants. (Further information and particulars of how to send and prepare samples and specimens may be had from The Director, R.H.S. Gardens, Wisley, Ripley, Surrey.)

The Fruit Garden Displayed (6s. 9d.) and *The Vegetable Garden Displayed* (3s. 10d.) are two admirable illustrated books which may be had from the R.H.S., in addition to certain inexpensive pamphlets on roses, herbaceous plants, shrubs, annuals, etc.

Specialist help may be had from the following kindred societies, whose addresses may be had from the Royal Horticultural Society:

Alpine Garden Society	Midland Daffodil Society
British Delphinium Society	National Auricula and Primula Society
British Fuchsia Society	National Cactus and Succulent Society
British Gladiolus Society	National Chrysanthemum Society
British Iris Society	National Dahlia Society
British National Carnation Society	National Rose Society
Cactus and Succulent Society of	National Sweet Pea Society
Great Britain	Scottish Rock Garden Club

THE LONDON GARDENS SOCIETY, 20 Buckingham Street, London, W.C.2, (minimum subscription 5s. a year). The Society will help to answer questions and, if possible, send an expert to advise on gardens.

THE MINISTRY OF AGRICULTURE AND FISHERIES publish advisory leaflets which may be obtained free on application to the Ministry at 9 Chester Terrace, London, N.W.1, or from H.M. Stationery Offices and booksellers.

COUNTY COUNCIL EDUCATION DEPARTMENTS often appoint Horticultural Officers who are willing to help private gardeners on problems of soil, fertilizers, plants and general cultivation.

THE CEMENT AND CONCRETE ASSOCIATION, 52 Grosvenor Gardens, London, S.W.1, supply free, on request, a number of garden construction sheets on how to make paving slabs, pools and garden frames.

CATALOGUES containing much cultural advice of value to the small gardener may be obtained from the following nurserymen, who sometimes make a small charge to meet the cost of production:

Blackmoor Nurseries, Liss, Hants. Descriptive fruit catalogue.

W. A. Constable Ltd., Southborough, Tunbridge Wells. Full cultural notes on lilies with descriptions.

Hillier & Sons, Winchester. Separate catalogues on many different categories of plant. These give details on habit, size, colour and flowering period.

T. Hilling & Co., Chobham, Woking, Surrey. Specialists in old-fashioned roses. Complete list available, also booklet on application (price 2s. 6d.) giving full descriptions and cultural notes.

W. E. Th. Ingwersen Ltd., Birch Farm Nursery, Gravetye, East Grinstead, Sussex. Full cultural notes and descriptions of alpine and rock garden plants.

Geo. Jackman & Son (Woking Nurseries) Ltd., Woking, Surrey. Their *Planter's Handbook* catalogue gives valuable cultural notes on all general nursery stock, including size, habit, colour and flowering period.

Laxton Bros. (Bedford) Ltd., 63 High Street, Bedford. Descriptive fruit catalogue.

R. C. Notcutt Ltd., Woodbridge, Suffolk. Particularly useful for trees, shrubs and roses.

Perry's Hardy Plant Farm, Enfield, Middlesex. Cultural notes on water lilies and aquatic plants.

John Scott & Co., The Royal Nurseries, Merriott, Somerset. General nursery stock and detailed cultural notes on alpines.

Six Hills Nursery Ltd., Stevenage, Herts. Detailed cultural notes and descriptions of alpines.

Stewart's Nurseries, Ferndown, Dorset. Cultural notes on water lilies and aquatic plants.

R. Wallace & Co., The Old Gardens, Tunbridge Wells. Especially informative on iris, lilies, water plants.

POTS. Two firms willing to make pots to special designs are:
C. H. Brannam Ltd., Litchdon Pottery, Barnstaple, Devon.
A. Harris & Sons, Farnham Potteries, Wrecclesham, Farnham, Surrey.

RIVIERA FENCING. Obtainable from Gerald Gilmer Ltd., Lewes, Sussex.